Charles H. Read Jr. MDCM

THIS NAVY DOCTOR
CAME ASHORE

ACORNPRESS

P.O. Box 22024
Charlottetown, Prince Edward Island
C1A 9J2
acornpresscanada.com

Printed and Bound in Canada
Cover and interior design by Matt Reid

Library and Archives Canada Cataloguing in Publication

Read, Charles H., 1918-
    This navy doctor came ashore / Charles H. Read Jr.

ISBN 978-1-894838-75-7

    1. Read, Charles H., 1918-. 2. Physicians--Prince Edward
Island--Biography. 3. Medicine, Rural--Prince Edward
Island--Anecdotes. I. Title.

R464.R42A3 2012   610.92   C2012-901249-1

Canada Council   Conseil des Arts
for the Arts   du Canada

The publisher acknowledges the support of the Government of Canada through the Canada Book Fund of the Department of Canadian Heritage and the Canada Council for the Arts Block Grant Program.

Charles H. Read Jr. MDCM

THIS NAVY DOCTOR
CAME ASHORE

The Acorn Press
Charlottetown
2012

This book is a memoir. The conversations in it were not tape-recorded, but reconstructed from my memory.

This book is presented in memory of my wonderful parents, Charles H. Read, Sr., and Nettie Gertrude Oulton.

I am most grateful to my first wife, Anne Greig, for her unwavering support throughout the events that are recorded in this book, and to my current wife, Chunghi Choo, for her support and encouragement during its writing.

I'm especially grateful to James McKean, MFA, PhD, whose advice and suggestions were important and made the writing of the book an ongoing pleasure.

PREFACE

On August 22, 1944, the ship I was in, HMS *Nabob*, Canada's first manned aircraft carrier, was so heavily damaged by a German torpedo in the Arctic Ocean north of Norway that she could not be repaired. By October, all of us Canadians who were lucky enough to have survived were back in Canada. I, who had been the junior medical officer and flight surgeon on *Nabob*, was in Ottawa for an appointment with the Medical Director General, Captain Archie McCallum. I expected he would want to talk with me about my experiences on *Nabob* and, especially, to discuss my next posting.

I'd thoroughly enjoyed being a flight surgeon and wanted to again be appointed to that position. I'd wondered if my chances of this happening would be improved if I took the American flight surgeon's course at Pensacola. Surely, I thought, Canada would be getting another aircraft carrier.

My first impression of Dr. McCallum was that he looked like a very relaxed older family doctor, one who had been in the navy for some time. Greeting me warmly, he said, "Well, Charlie, have a seat and tell me what you would like to do next."

That he knew my first name wasn't a surprise because his reputation was that he knew the names of all 400-plus doctors in the navy. But I was disappointed when he didn't first ask about my experiences on *Nabob*; apparently he was not interested in anything about my past, only my future. Perhaps he didn't know I'd been a flight surgeon, or perhaps he didn't even know that there was such a position.

"Well, sir," I said, "I've had the British course in Aviation Medicine and since then I've had considerable experience as the flight surgeon on *Nabob*. I enjoyed that tremendously. Now I'd like more of it. If I were to take the American flight surgeon's course at Pensacola, I'd be really prepared for a posting to another carrier."

His response was immediate and decisive. "The navy has no interest in sending anyone to Pensacola. What's your second choice?"

Again I was disappointed. The tone of his voice implied that was that, no further discussion. These were not the words or tone of a relaxed older doctor, but rather those of a busy executive who had a little problem to solve and wanted to get on with it.

Realizing that my career as a flight surgeon was finished, I began to think. I had been to sea and was unlikely to get another seagoing appointment. The war was winding down, so where would I like to quietly fight the rest of it? Then I remembered how much I'd enjoyed the three weeks I'd spent in Charlottetown during the Christmas holidays of 1943 when I relieved the medical officer at HMCS Queen Charlotte. This city of 20,000, in which this landship was "moored," was much to my liking, perhaps because I'd grown up in Amherst, Nova Scotia, just across the Northumberland Strait, where the culture, I thought, was very similar. Also, I knew that I would be the only medical officer, that I already knew the personnel, that I'd have a lot of independence, significant responsibility, and virtual freedom from naval protocol and politics. One couldn't ask for more.

"Sir, I've thought it over. I'd like to go to HMCS Queen Charlotte in Charlottetown, Prince Edward Island."

"Good," he said. "Report there in one week."

CHAPTER ONE

Just eleven months previous I'd only been in the navy about two weeks and was working happily in the dockyard sick bay at HMCS Stadacona in Halifax. Suddenly I was ordered to go to Charlottetown to relieve their medical officer, who'd been granted a three-week Christmas leave. All I was told was, "He's the only Doc there."

The next morning, I was on my way. By that evening, when our train arrived at the ferry terminal at Cape Tormentine, New Brunswick, I'd been well filled in by the other passengers on how active the German submarines had been in the Gulf of St. Lawrence, just north of the Island, in the past few months. Several ships had been torpedoed, they said, one quite recently. So I probably shouldn't have been surprised when, just before our ferry, the SS *Charlottetown*, left its moorings, the loud hailer blared, "This is the captain speaking. Because we have been advised an enemy submarine is active in this area, I recommend that if you still want to go with us, you stay on deck near the lifeboats. That is all."

Obviously we were in a war zone. However, with the temperature near zero (F) and a north wind blowing briskly, all of us passengers chose to accept whatever increased risk there might be by staying in the warmth of the lounge. A few sat in the chairs; most of us walked around more or less aimlessly; some paced up and down; and a few chose to chat. Fortunately the hour-long passage to Borden, Prince Edward Island, passed without incident.

The next morning in Charlottetown, the concierge at the Charlottetown Hotel gave me directions to the naval base. "It's only five blocks away," he said. "Go straight down Kent Street – that's the one right in front of the hotel – until you come to Hillsborough Street. Early in the war, the Royal Canadian Navy bought a three-storey brick building. That's now HMCS Queen Charlotte. You're going to be the medical officer there, you said?"

"Yes, but just for three weeks. I'm looking forward to being here for the holidays."

I had no trouble recognizing the naval base because I soon saw the White Ensign flying from a tall flagpole near the entrance. Immediately I was piped "on board," and the Officer of the Day took me to meet the commanding officer, Lieut. Cdr. Charles MacKenzie. Of average height, he had a reddish acne-scarred face, a receding hairline, a booming voice, a gruff mien, and an artificial leg, the result of a shipboard accident earlier in the war. I soon learned he had a good sense of humour, a warm heart, and very good relations with his crew.

After welcoming me, he said, "How long have you been in the navy?"

"Just three weeks. I've been lucky so far. I'm from Nova Scotia and my first posting was to HMCS Stadacona in Halifax where I've been working in the Dockyard Clinic. And then, two days ago, Surgeon Lieut. Cdr. Chapman called me to his office and informed me that I was to spend the Christmas holidays here. I was surprised and delighted he chose me. I thought it'd be a lot like home. You see, I grew up in Amherst, Nova Scotia, and, as you know, that's not far away."

"Good. Join me in the wardroom later and we can have a drink before lunch. That'll give us a chance to have a good visit."

My office and the sick bay were on the third floor. There I met the two Sick Bay Attendants (SBAs or Tiffies), the senior being Petty Officer Carl Perry. I soon realized they were experienced, medically knowledgeable, and reliable. That they were great friends was easy to tell and they told me they'd lived together for two or three years.

When I asked about the crew, they said that it consisted of about thirty officers and men and about three hundred new recruits who were here for their basic training. They'd come from all across Canada and all of them were volunteers, between eighteen and twenty years of age. Most were away from home for the first time.

Those numbers I remember very clearly, because the very next morning I found on my desk two pads measuring three inches by five, each containing two hundred printed forms. They reminded me of prescription pads, but not like any I'd ever seen before. On the top line the print read: "To the Retail Vendor at _____ in _____ County," under which was: "This is to certify that I am attending professionally" and under that a space for a name, a street number, and name and town. The next line was: "and he/she requires _____ for medicinal use only and not as a beverage." The last line was one for the day, the month, and the year, and finally on the lowest line for the physician's signature.

I picked up the phone. "Carl. Come tell me what the hell these two pads are that you've put on my desk, and what I'm supposed to do with them."

Carl arrived promptly, a big smile on his face. "These, sir, are scripts. I'm afraid you're supposed to sign them, all four hundred."

I looked at him in surprise.

He continued. "We're a bit behind the rest of the country here. We still have prohibition. To get any wine or beer or spirits here, you have to be 'sick.' You have to go to your doctor and ask him for one of the scripts. Then you take it to the government-owned liquor store, officially called the 'vendor,' where you buy whatever kind of liquor that's written on the script. Of course, the vendor keeps track of what you buy to make sure you're not sick too often.

The prohibitionists are very concerned about the health of our citizens."

He delivered this last phrase with a smile.

This was my introduction to a unique feature of being a physician here: automatically I had a significant role in the province's liquor control system. Carl told me that each month all the doctors received these blank prescription pads. The presumed ailing possessor could then take the completed script to the Government Liquor Store and buy whatever he/she had chosen. It was the only legal way one could obtain liquids containing alcohol. It being Christmastime, I realized I had a very serious responsibility.

As I started to sign, I thought, "Thank God I have a short name." Two hundred signatures later, I decided that was enough for one sitting and went down one floor to the wardroom. Only the CO was there, sitting at a table by the window. When I entered he looked around and said, "Come join me, Read. Have a drink?"

"Thanks, I could use one, sir. I've just finished signing half of those bloody scripts. There's another two hundred to do after lunch. A Molson's would be great. Thanks a lot."

The CO looked amused as he nodded to the wine

steward and soon my beer appeared. "By the way," he said, "we're not very formal here, so call me by my first name. It's Charlie."

"Thanks and mine is Charles. But tell me about these scripts. I thought prohibition was a thing of the past."

"Not on Prince Edward Island. We were the first province to have prohibition and the only one to still have it."

"The first one on and the only one not off. How come?"

"Well, back about the turn of the century, the women in Charlottetown became upset because there was so much drunkenness and so many saloons in the city. It's said there were 140, one for every 70 citizens. The women, even though they didn't have a vote, organized vigorously and got the legislature to pass the Prohibition Act. In the beginning that was only for this city, but six years later the whole damn province was dry. Up to then, rum had always been the favourite drink. Since then, it and other hard liquors have been legally available only for 'medical and religious purposes' and that required a medical doctor's prescription. That's something we find both a nuisance and damn annoying."

He finished his drink and ordered another.

"I can't imagine that the doctors are very enthusiastic about their role in controlling the supply of liquor," I commented.

"No, I don't think they are, but they pretty much have to in order to look after their patients. Most of them give the scripts to their patients, but some sell them. That's how the speakeasies get their supply."

"Speakeasies, here?"

"You look surprised, but there are quite a few of them, as well as bootleggers. Sometimes you can find them tucked in behind lunch counters. I've heard that if you want a drink, just tell your taxi driver. And the gossip is that there are quite a few very respectable ladies, especially widows with no visible means of support, who are quite happy to serve thirsty customers in the privacy of their parlours. So you see, there's quite a lot of places to slake one's thirst.

"Until the war began in 1939, the rumrunners supplied the Island very adequately. Then the only reason we needed a script was for beer and it wasn't very popular anyway. But with the war came the end of the rumrunners and cheap liquor. Prohibition became real. They say all the rumrunners joined the navy."

He looked at his watch. "Sorry, but I've got to go. My wife will have lunch ready and she doesn't like for me to be late." I knew there was a lot more to the story, but it was clear that was all I was to hear at that time.

Within a few days my wife joined me, and, as a special treat for dinner that night, she prepared a special meal – fried cod. At my home in Nova Scotia I had eaten salt cod, but only after it had been soaked first to remove the salt and then mixed with potato and fried as a fish cake, usually for breakfast. My mother never served fresh cod because she considered it too coarse a fish. So when Anne placed fried salt cod before me I was surprised, for I had never seen such a dish before. My first taste surprised me even more. Salt! Back to the plate it went. It was obvious that Anne, who grew up in Ontario, hadn't known that salt cod had to be desalted before it was served. But after a beer or two, we both had a good laugh. "Salt cod" became one of our inside jokes, and she stood up to the kidding nicely. We thoroughly enjoyed the third-floor apartment on Kent Street rented to us by the doctor and his wife who had gone on leave.

My medical duties were not arduous and the local doctors, especially Dr. Seaman and Dr. MacKenzie, whom I met at the Prince Edward Island Hospital, were most welcoming and cooperative. While most of our social activities involved the other officers and their wives, I also soon met and socialized with a number of the personnel assigned to the Royal Air Force Navex (Navigation School) located at the new Charlottetown airport. One of the pilots, Flight Lieut. Adrian Quito, a veteran of many Coastal Command sorties, asked me if I would like to fly a Navex exercise with him. I'd had only two flights before: the first in 1936 in an open cockpit Tiger Moth at the former Upton Airport in Charlottetown, and the other in 1938 in a Boeing Stratoliner on the flight from Chicago Midway to Minneapolis. So this offer sounded very exciting and I quickly said, "Sure." However, when I learned we were going to fly in an Anson V, I lost some of my enthusiasm. This was a twin-engine aircraft that RAF Bomber Command used briefly at the beginning of the war. I thought of them as outdated and the fabric coating on such a large aircraft did not increase my confidence. But this is what Navex was using, so I told myself they must be reliable.

Sitting in the co-pilot's seat beside Adrian, with ten or so students behind us in individual seats, I felt reasonably relaxed. We flew up and down the Northumberland Strait that separated Prince Edward Island from Nova Scotia and New Brunswick while I tried to identify the various capes, bays, and other landmarks that I'd known since childhood. I found that difficult. After several hours, we had completed our exercise and turned towards our base.

But when we began our final approach and Adrian tried to lower the wheels in preparation for landing, a red signal light on the instrument panel came on. "What's that mean?" I asked.

"That shows the port wheel has not come down. Not a big problem, so don't worry."

But I did. A wheels-up landing – I'd read about them. I felt my pulse pick up. Maybe I was going to have a short career in the navy. I tightened my seat-belt a notch and looked behind me to see what the students were doing. All appeared unusually alert.

Adrian aborted the landing and we flew in circles around Charlottetown as he carried out various manoeuvres to try to correct the problem, as well as dispose of any extra fuel. The red light stayed on. Below I saw the fire equipment arrive and begin to spread foam on the landing strip. Several ambulances lined up. That didn't do anything to relieve my anxiety, but at least they were ready for us. Then we got word from the ground that the wheel was down, but was it fixed in place? Would it collapse on landing?

Adrian appeared very calm, very businesslike. He acted as if he knew exactly how to handle this situation. Finally he said, "Okay, we're going in now."

Now I felt calm, although very alert, and I noticed my heart was beating more rapidly than usual as we approached the ground. Adrian held the aircraft's attitude so that the starboard wheel was slightly below the port one. Finally we touched down, landing on our starboard wheel. Then, after rolling a considerable distance, he leveled the aircraft so the port wheel came in touch with the ground. It didn't collapse and we rolled to a routine stop. A faulty signal light had been the problem.

Afterwards we had a beer. "It always tastes especially good after a 'hairy do,'" he said. We became very good friends.

Later I thought about what that experience had meant to me. Yes, it was exciting and I had felt considerable anxiety, but I had been able to cope with the risk calmly, just feeling unusually alert. I'd also realized how much confidence I had in my pilot and his ability to cope with the problem, although I'd been but a short time a member of his team.

Of course Anne and I were expected to attend the New Year's Eve party to welcome 1944 at the Charlottetown Hotel. The province being dry, visible consumption of alcoholic beverages was unlawful. But in the rooms rented by the partygoers, hard liquor flowed freely, although wine and beer were nowhere to be seen. Just before midnight, my wife and I got in the elevator to go down to the ballroom. We didn't know any of our fellow travelers, but all of them were unusually talkative and friendly. Halfway down, the elevator suddenly stopped, clearly between floors. None of the buttons we pushed caused a response. No one answered the telephone. Nobody panicked, but one man said, "What a hell of a way to start the New Year." Maybe I said that.

There was only one way out: the escape hatch in the ceiling. Nobody was dressed appropriately for that kind of exercise – the women in their high heels and long dresses, the men in tuxedos or in their dress uniforms. I was the youngest in the group, and the slimmest, so I volunteered. I took off my shoes and jacket and, with help from the others, managed to climb onto the shoulders of one of the men, opened the hatch, clambered onto the roof of the elevator, and pushed open the door to the floor above. From there, I called the hotel's mechanic who soon arrived and solved the problem. We missed the midnight celebration.

CHAPTER TWO

These events from the year before passed through my head in the late October day of 1944 when my wife and I arrived in Charlottetown once again. The city was the financial and commercial centre of Prince Edward Island. Its population consisted largely of the descendants of the original Scots, Irish, and Acadians. We quickly found a nicely furnished flat that we shared with a young woman whose husband was a dentist in the Canadian Army in France.

Throughout the war, HMCS Queen Charlotte had served as base where new recruits, usually about four hundred at any one time, came for their initial naval training and indoctrination. The staff officers and the ship's crew were the same as when I was here almost a year previously. My office in the land-based ship was still on the third floor near the sick bay, where the two very pleasant and capable sick berth attendants, Carl Perry and Richard MacDonald, had long been established and seemed to be pleased that I'd returned. Our Commanding Officer was still the same, Lieut. Cdr. Charles MacKenzie. He'd lost his leg in a shipboard accident earlier in the war and stomped around on his artificial leg, very much in charge. He soon demonstrated that he could down three triple gins before lunch and show no signs of it. The atmosphere on the ship showed he ran a "good ship" and a happy one. Both he and his wife, Ruth, welcomed us back.

To my surprise, the core officers were the same as when I was there before. The Schoolie, Lieut. Charles Silliphant, from Summerside, a former high school math teacher, was his usual warm self and always had the latest news on horse-racing and trout-fishing spots. Lieut. Ian Burnett, a native Charlottetonian with contacts with the major local newspaper, was a quiet competent man. I think

Lieut. Langford, some years older than the rest of us, was from Campbell River, British Columbia. His stories always aroused in me visions of gold mining and life on the frontier, all probably incorrect, for I didn't know that Campbell River was on Vancouver Island, not in the interior of the mainland.

We also had a mascot, a boxer dog. He impressed me when one time he got a cut on a front paw. Coming to the front door of the barracks, he was allowed in as usual. Thereupon he, walking on three legs, came directly up to my third-floor office and sat there holding his hurt paw off the floor, waiting for my attention.

I'd enjoyed this group when I was there at Christmastime in 1943 and was happy to be with them again.

CHAPTER THREE

Not long after I'd come on board and just before the current class of recruits were to finish, Naval Headquarters in Ottawa announced that no more recruits were needed. The Canadian Navy had grown from a total of 2,500 officers and men in 1939 to 100,000 in 1944, all volunteers except for a relatively few permanent forces and transfers from the merchant marine. It was the largest percentage increase of any military service in the world. By now it was clear the war on the sea was winding down, the German U-boat menace was rapidly declining, and the Canadian Navy, consisting of corvettes, frigates, and a few destroyers built for the North Atlantic, would not be of much use in the Pacific.

For me, the reduced number of recruits meant that instead of having three or four hundred young men to care for, I'd have twenty or thirty, all young and healthy. It looked to me as if my professional life was going to be pretty boring. I'd have to make some plans, perhaps ask for a new posting.

Just a few days before the last of the recruits left, the CO called me to his office. Seemingly unusually tense, he leaned forward across the deck as he began to talk. "Charles, there's a situation in Eldon I want to tell you about. It's a small village twenty-five miles east of here with a number of smaller settlements around it, like Orwell, Pinette, Flat River, Uigg, Belfast, and Roseberry. In that whole region, there's no doctor for the first time ever. Twenty-five miles further on, in Murray River, there's one, but he's seventy years old and not that well. You may not know that once you're outside of the city there's no paved roads, just gravel or clay, so that makes travel a little more difficult for them. But if you were to go down there a couple of times a week, it would be a godsend for these people and good publicity for the navy. So how would you like to set up a family practice in Eldon, say on Wednesday and Saturday afternoons? You can have the use of the navy panel truck at no cost. You might just find it an interesting experience and you certainly would supply a much-needed service for the people in that area."

He looked at me expectantly, quietly tapping his desk with a pencil.

It took me no time at all to decide. A country doctor, no less. Not a role that was in my plans for the future, but I might well have experiences I would not otherwise have had, and it would be a real opportunity to help these people; there seemed no question about their need. Sounded really interesting.

"Yes, sir, I'd like to do that very much."

The CO looked pleased by my response as he smiled, got up, and shook my hand.

I wondered whether he had permission from naval headquarters to do this, perhaps as a public relations ploy. More likely, I decided, he'd heard of the plight of these people and decided to let humanity and common sense outweigh regulations. After all, he was the captain of this "ship" and that gave him considerable power.

When I got home I told my wife, Anne, about this. Immediately she was fully on board with the idea. The very next day I drove to Eldon and introduced myself to Annie, the person the CO had suggested might have a room in her house, which I could use as an office. Of course she had: her front parlour for ten dollars per month. (I think it had all been arranged before I ever got there. Later I learned she and my CO had been friends for many years.) The location was ideal because it was the first house on the Belfast Road that branches off from the main highway to the Wood Islands ferry, which goes to Nova Scotia. A charming woman in her late sixties, Annie was an alert, grey-haired, bosomy, a little broad-in-the-beam, grandmotherly woman, who valued quality over style. She was also a good cook.

I quickly recognized that she knew everyone in the area and soon was filling me in on each patient, even advising me how much to charge. "You can't tell how much they're worth by how they're dressed." She once told me in her best Scottish accent, "Some of the tightwads around here get dressed in their oldest clothes when they go to see the doctor, so he'll be thinkin' they don't have any money, especially if the doctor be young and fresh out of school."

She greeted each patient as he or she came to her kitchen door, and chatted with them in her kitchen as they waited to see me. Sometimes she tried to help, or possibly she was just being friendly, by asking questions like, "Och aye, Marty (the owner of the General Store), and how would ye'd be t'dy? Is it the yaller janders ye'd be having?"

I had some difficulty deciding on appropriate fees. I continued to wear my uniform and, of course, was being paid by the navy, so I wasn't dependent on what I made in this practice. On the other hand, I believed that when people paid for services, they valued them more than if they were entirely free. Finally I decided that I would charge three dollars for a complete history and physical examination. A token amount, of course, but they were already helping pay my salary with their taxes and these fees were not essential to my well-being.

From my previous experience at HMCS Queen Charlotte, I knew that one of the first things I had to do was to arrange for the item every physician in Prince Edward Island needed: scripts. That I did with a telephone call, but I was a little disappointed when they sent me only twenty-five each month. I'd thought I'd need many more than that, but it turned out I always had plenty. Many of my patients must have been teetotalers, or they had other and possibly less expensive ways to get their jollies, I thought. I soon found this to be true.

CHAPTER FOUR

From the beginning I had a number of patients each time I was at my office. It didn't take me long to notice that most of their complaints were not of much significance and might have been saved up over a number of months. I wondered if they were using them as an excuse to get a close-up look at the new doctor, especially one who wore a navy uniform. One of them was a man in his fifties whose wife said that he snored. He said he wasn't tired the next day and didn't fall asleep during the afternoon or any other time. However his tonsils were enlarged and he was obese. I recommended he lose weight and that he also see the ear, nose, and throat doctor at the Polyclinic in Charlottetown. Another complained that her fingernails sometimes split. I assured her that that was not a sign of calcium deficiency. Failing to find the cause of many complaints, I did my best to make sure I listened intently to whatever they had to say and to respond in what I thought an appropriate way. In a very short time, I learned that it wasn't enough to take a thorough history, do a complete physical examination, and to discuss their problems with them, whether they be physical, marital, emotional, or financial. I decided I had to add something more. I talked with the owner of a pharmacy close to HMCS Queen Charlotte and made a deal to buy multivitamin tablets from him at a low price. From that time on, while my patients still seemed unenthusiastic about paying my basic three-dollar fee, they visibly brightened up when I began to add on ten dollars for the hundred multivitamin capsules that I began to dispense each visit. I decided it must be important for them to have something tangible to show for having gone to see the doctor. From that time on, I made sure they never left my office empty-handed. They even began coming back to my office to get refills. "I feel so much better since I started taking them," they said.

Talking and the "laying on of hands" were not quite enough.

CHAPTER FIVE

About three weeks after I opened my office, the telephone rang just as the last patient was leaving. Annie answered and called out, "It's for you, Doctor. It's a man and he sounds scared." Then she passed the phone to me.

The first words I heard were, "Doc, yah gotta come quick. It's an emergency." The high pitch of his voice, spoken while inhaling, underlined this man's anxiety. "Please calm down," I said, putting as much warmth and confidence in my voice as I could muster under the circumstances. "Now, speak slowly and tell me about your problem."

He seemed a bit calmer when he continued. "It's my son. He drank some kerosene. Now he's unconscious and he's having trouble breathing..."

"Make sure there's nothing in his mouth that's clogging his breathing. Where do you live?"

"We live in Uigg. Annie can tell you how to get here. And, for God's sake, Doc, hurry!"

Although I'd never been to Uigg, I knew it wasn't too far away. Annie knew the family and where they lived and gave m e what turned out to be accurate directions. "They're good, simple people," she said, as I ran out the door, "and they're not much for talking."

Driving the navy van as fast as I dared on the narrow red clay road, immense clouds of dust rising behind me, finding the family in Uigg was the least of my problems. The more significant one was that I'd never heard of kerosene poisoning. I was familiar with kerosene, because during every summer of my childhood we used kerosene lamps to light our cottage. The daily replenishing of the lamps with kerosene and cleaning the glass chimneys were a never-ending chore. But drinking the stuff? I'd never heard of anyone doing that. More importantly,

I hadn't learned anything about kerosene poisoning in medical school. I had no idea why the boy was unconscious or what the treatment was for this kind of poisoning.

I drove in the lane and parked near the gate beside a rather dilapidated tractor. The house was typical of so many of the farmhouses on Prince Edward Island: white painted clapboard, a centrally positioned door, and a steeply pitched roof so the snow would slide off easily. Only the dog greeted me. It came charging toward me, intermittently barking and growling and acting in a very inhospitable fashion. As I walked across the hundred or so feet of lawn to the house, I avoided eye contact with him but still kept track of where he was. I kept talking quietly to him, "Look dog, I'm coming here to help a little boy. I'm really a good guy, so don't get in my way." Little by little he paid somewhat less attention to me, but I continued to feel he was ever threatening. At last I reached the safety of the front porch and knocked on the door. I braced myself for what might come next.

A tall, lean, dark-haired man, who looked to be in his early thirties, opened the door and said, "God, I thought you'd never get here."

I didn't reply, for even as I entered I saw the patient. He was lying supine on a sofa on the opposite side of the room, directly across from the door. Although he must have been close to twenty feet away, I could hear his loud and laboured breathing. When I reached his side, I saw that his skin was dusky, his lips were blue, and that that he was struggling to breathe. First I made sure that there was nothing in his mouth that could be impeding his breathing. I really didn't need to use a stethoscope to listen to his chest, because I could easily hear the loud bubbling sounds without it. It told me there was a lot of fluid in his bronchi. Examining some of the fluid in his mouth showed me it contained a lot of mucus. When I found his blood pressure was normal, I was relieved. Actually, apart from his breathing difficulty, he looked like a very healthy four-year-old boy.

But what to do? The few medicines I carried in my bag were not going to help this situation. The one obvious finding was the fluid and mucus in his bronchi, in which he seemed to be drowning. So I picked him up by his feet, allowing his head to rest lightly on the sofa. Immediately he began to drain copious amounts of fluid from his mouth and nose. This went on and on, I don't really know for how long. He showed no sign of regaining consciousness, but he certainly was getting rid of a lot of the kind of liquid mucus that accounted for what I'd heard in his lungs.

Across the room, not far from the door, the several members of his family huddled silently on a sofa. I had the feeling that the family was becoming restive, as this treatment to them must have seemed anything but spectacular, not at all using any of the magic often expected of doctors. While they could see the continuing drainage, neither they nor I could see much improvement. But, by this time, I thought he perhaps was not draining as much, but maybe that was wishful thinking related to my having become very tired holding what was probably a forty-pound boy up by his feet for this length of time. Finally I had to lay the boy down on the sofa. Certainly his breathing was not as laboured or as noisy as it was and his lips were not as blue.

I wondered what else I could do. Without any ex-pectation of success, I reached in my bag and pulled out a bottle of one-half per cent neo-synephrine nose drops, the well-known decongestant that we all have used when we had a cold. I thought maybe this might clear his nose of mucus. Anyway, I squeezed several drops in each nostril. To my amazement, he almost immediately came to, opened his eyes, and sat up, his breathing essentially normal.

I immediately did another physical. His lungs were almost clear and he seemed to have largely returned to normal. He knew his name, his age, what day it was, and he talked like a normal four-year-old boy.

I had the feeling that the family was no more impressed with what I had done than I. They neither thanked me nor even showed me to the door. On my way back to my vehicle even the dog ignored me.

All I had done was to help him get rid of the fluid he had in his lungs. It was all I knew to do. To me, treating the symptoms made sense and I think it helped him. At least I had no reason to believe I had done harm.

The family never offered to pay me and I didn't feel I'd done enough to justify sending a bill. I think it was the only case I ever had in which nobody said a word. But I learned how a whole family could panic when faced with a situation in which they feel helpless.

When I got back to Annie's, I said, "You said they don't do much talking. I'd like to modify that. They don't do any talking." Then I told her the whole story. Annie just shook her head.

CHAPTER SIX

I'd been told that before I would be accepted
as a part of the community, I probably would
be tested. So not long after the kerosene poisoning, it happened. After looking after the last of my
afternoon's clients, I made a house call to see the
daughter of one of the leading citizens in the community, a deacon in the Presbyterian Church. After
I finished looking after his daughter, he invited me
to stay a while and have a drink. In a few minutes
his wife appeared with elegant cut glasses and placed
them on the table before us. They looked like glasses
partially filled with water, but when she asked

whether I would like to mix it with Coke or ginger ale, I gathered it was not water; it tasted a lot like the ethyl alcohol that we had learned a little about in college days. After we chatted for a while, my host said, "How do you like the drink?"

I really hadn't liked it any more than I did when we experimented with it in college days, but of course I said, "It's very good. Where did you ever get it?"

He looked me up and down as if he was deciding whether I could be trusted. Then he said, "Come with me."

We left the house and went out to the barn. In it on one side were about a dozen stalls for milking cows. On the other side there were two huge Clydesdales and two other horses that I thought he might use for harness racing. Looking up I saw the loft was filled with the winter's supply of hay. Near the far end was a pile of horse manure. This is where we stopped. My host picked up a pitchfork and with a few deft strokes removed the manure, exposing a trap door. After he opened it, we went down a ladder to a large, well-lit room. On the cement floor I noticed several bags of sugar and a pile of potatoes. But what really caught my attention was the large still.

"Wow!" I said. "This is as impressive as your product. Obviously you've been doing this for some time. Do many of your friends make 'shine,' too?"

"I'm sure you know the old saying, 'ask me no questions and I'll tell you no lies, ask me no questions and there'll be no good-byes.'"

This he said with a certain frostiness in his voice and I recognized I had overstepped. He had been testing me and I was not yet wholly accepted as one of them.

Then he went on. "We've had this here prohibition for a long time, so years ago we decided to look after things for ourselves. We don't sell any; we do give some to our friends and use it for socializing. It's real convenient. Of course, a number of our friends and neighbours know what we're up to, but they know how to keep their mouths shut. I'm sure you will, too."

I detected a hint of a warning in his voice as he said that. "You can depend on me," I said quickly. "And thanks for showing me your set-up. Everyone knows there's a lot of shine being made. The other day I noticed in *The Guardian* that the consumption of sugar on the Island is higher than in any other province, even though it's the smallest in population.

I'm sure it's not all being used on breakfast cereal or for making jam."

"That's for sure. Most everyone I know is making wine or beer. I'd be glad to give you a bottle to take home."

"Sure, that would be great. I've really enjoyed my visit with you. Thanks for the shine. Oh, I'm sure your daughter will be fine in the morning."

(I never did tell him I poured it out on the road not far from his place. No use taking the chance of the Mounties stopping me for something and finding shine in the doctor's navy vehicle.)

A few days later, a navy officer home on leave – whose father was the chief of police – invited me to his home. After a time I asked him if I could use the bathroom. While there, I thought I smelled a faint odour of juniper berries and then I noticed that the bathtub was partially filled with what looked like water. Thinking all that unusual, I asked him about it. He laughed and said, "Oh that's my father for you. He's always into something. He has a group of friends who get together about once a week to play poker. Just now they have a little competition going amongst them to see who can make the best bathtub gin. What you saw was dad's most recent production.

I hope you didn't pull the plug out."

I assured him I hadn't, but I thought that if even the chief of police was into making illicit liquor, it must be pretty generally accepted as being okay. No wonder the Islanders were using so much sugar.

At dinner that night I was thinking about this script thing and told my wife about the still and the police chief. Because she was from Ontario, this kind of goings-on was new to her. Not so to me. I said, "I've told you about our cottage at Tidnish on the bay that separates Nova Scotia and New Brunswick, and how on a clear, calm day we could see Prince Edward Island. Not an active water for boats of any kind; a motor boat going by was an event. From the time I was eight years old, I used to sleep on a hammock on the verandah facing the water. Sometimes, especially on moonless lights, the sound of a motorboat traveling at high speed would awaken me and I'd see lights far out on the water flashing intermittently. I was sure they were signals. Sometimes I even saw what I thought were answering ones on the far shore. Rumours abounded. Someone was said to have seen Mounties chasing a truck laden with boxes, or that there had been a big landing up the shore near Northport the previous night.

"One time I overheard my father talking to a close friend about rumrunning. He was telling about a man in Port Elgin. Apparently he had two fast boats that he used to land liquor at various places up and down the coast. Hearing comments like these, my imagination had no difficulty in conjuring up lots of exciting scenarios."

My wife interjected, "You must have had a great time."

"Sure did. It was really exciting. Even back then I knew that rumrunning was against the law, but nobody thought that it was wrong. 'Illegal, but not immoral,' it was called. This was probably because big-time gangsters were not a part of the game, as they were in the Boston States. I never heard of anyone getting hurt and rarely did anyone get caught. If they did, there was a quick trial and they were soon out of jail."

Back at Queen Charlotte the next morning, I found my new supply of scripts had arrived, so I signed about half of them and then went to see Schoolie, knowing he was an Islander and would probably know something about these scripts.

"Oh," he said, smiling. "They're a damn nuisance, but you get used to them. Actually, they've only been a factor since the war began. Until then, we all got our liquor from rumrunners. Everyone had a keg stashed away somewhere handy. Why, before the previous owners of this very building handed it over to the navy, they had to see that the renters of several of the rooms on the ground floor had removed the rum stored in them. It was that available. Better stuff and a lot cheaper than we get now from the government liquor store."

"Didn't the government try to stop this inflow of illegal liquor?"

Schoolie laughed. "It depends on your point of view. The prohibitionists, who felt that liquor was the 'source of all evil,' thought the government's efforts were halfhearted at best. Certainly they were ineffective. That's not too surprising with a population that had lived for many years under prohibition and still imbibed. They didn't care where or how they got their liquor. I remember reading that bootlegging and rumrunning were occupations that, while not respectable, at least were necessary. Another person wrote prohibition meant not allowing your neighbour to have a drink."

"Hasn't anyone tried to get the law changed?" I asked.

"Oh sure. I think it was in 1927 that the Conservatives had as a major plank that they would introduce government control if elected. The prohibitionists were outraged and stumped against them, essentially turning it into a moral crusade. The Liberals stood back, suggesting only they would have another plebiscite, but laying the evils of drink at the Conservatives' door. The Tories got only six of the thirty seats. Two years later, the plebiscite promised by the Grits was the last great prohibitionists' victory in Canada. A leading national 'dry' publication noted, 'the tight little island' stood the test. I don't know whether the double entendre was a mistake or not. I remember another writer commenting 'the Islanders went thirsty only by choice.'"

"Well, Schoolie, I guess that just means I have to keep on signing. Let's go to the wardroom and have a drink."

CHAPTER SEVEN

We celebrated Christmas and New Year's Eve much as we had the previous year, with many returning naval officers making Queen Charlotte their social headquarters. There was no shortage of scripts. One afternoon Anne and I were invited out to North River Road where a second cousin of mine, Stewart Jones, who owned twelve acres of land, allowed us to cut down a lovely symmetrical balsam fir for our Christmas tree. There were the usual New Year's parties, and the elevator in the Charlottetown Hotel caused us no trouble.

The weather in the winter so far had been remarkable because of a complete lack of snow, making my travel in the panel truck to Eldon very normal. But the forecast for Saturday, January 20, promised to change my travel plans. "Twenty inches of snow beginning about noon, with high winds." In other words, a blizzard was brewing. The forecast looked to be accurate because by noon it was snowing and snowing hard. Looking out the window of my office, I watched the wind-driven flakes fly by. On the ground, snow devils were swirling. Drifts were beginning to form. I walked down to the wardroom on the second floor and ran into Schoolie. "It looks like the forecast is right on target. I won't be making my trip to Eldon today, not in this storm. I'm going to go home and have lunch with my wife and then I'm going to make a fire in the fireplace and curl up on our sofa with Hans Zinsser's new memoir, *As I Remember Him*."

I'd hardly said this when the telephone rang. It was for me. "Hello." I knew my voice showed the irritation I felt. Damn, I can't ever let my voice sound like that.

The male voice on the other end of the line said, "Dr. Read?" in a high-pitched voice. He sounded anxious.

"Yes, this is Dr. Read." I hoped now my voice sounded warm and confident. "How may I help you?"

"Doctor, it's my wife. She had a baby nine days ago, and now her right breast is red, swollen, and painful. Her temperature is 102 degrees F. Will you come to see her? She's very sick."

"Where do you live?"

Thoughts and feelings intermingled in my head. "Sounds like a breast abscess, she needs attention, it'll be hell going anywhere the way this storm is shaping up, I don't want to go, I have to go, it was going to be such a satisfying afternoon, damn it to hell."

"We live in Roseberry. Doc, you gotta come. She's real sick." He sounded desperate.

"My God, man. Roseberry's four miles beyond Eldon and that's twenty-four miles from here, and there's a blizzard that's already started. I'd never able to make it. She's not even a patient of mine. Who's her doctor, anyway? Why didn't you call him?"

"I know she's not your patient. Dr. Yeo delivered her, but he said he'd never be able to get here. He said to call you because you're young and you're the only doc who's got a snowmobile."

I was silent for a moment as I thought more about it. Even though she'd not been my patient, I knew I'd have to go. This woman needed help and I was a doctor. I also knew I was the only doctor to have a chance of getting there in this storm. The man didn't know, though, that in my silence, I'd decided to go. He pleaded, "Please, Doc. You can go anywhere in that snowmobile of yours."

"I wish that was true," I replied. "The name is wrong. That machine is not mobile in the snow. But I'll do my best to help you. We'll leave as soon as we can."

The old panel truck I usually drove was of no use at all on newly snow-covered gravel roads, so I called the Mobil Oil Company. Earlier in the month that company had called me and, as a public service, put at my disposal their snowmobile and their driver. One of the first models made by Bombardier, it looked like an efficient machine, a half-track, with skis in the front, a wood-paneled pear-shaped body, folding bucket seats in front and a foam rubber bench in the rear, windshield wipers, and a good heater. But with more than two or three inches of new snow, it was useless. The oil company used it to service their oil rig on frozen Hillsborough Bay, but that meant traveling on board ice, not soft snow.

First of all I called Annie and told her about what I proposed to do, and why. She replied, "Oh, it's a terrible storm that's a cumin'," her Scottish accent clearly evident. "Do be careful. I'll be waiting for you whenever you get here, night or day."

I went home, and told my wife what I was planning to do.

"Do you really have to go? This is a terrible storm. Isn't it pretty risky? Do you think it's safe?"

"I don't want to go, but this woman really needs help and I'm the only doctor who is in a position to go. We'll be okay."

After I had some lunch I put on my long johns and heavy pants, a flannel shirt and two wool sweaters, the fleece-lined flying boots Bobby Bradshaw, the Squadron Leader of 852 on *Nabob*, had given me, and an old raccoon coat handed down from my father. I was ready when Tim Ryan, a relative new-comer from Texas, arrived with the snowmobile. A tall, rangy, competent man, he was the foreman of the oil well Mobil was drilling out in the bay. With him was another Texan, Bill White – short, heavy-set, and jovial, who worked for Tim as a roustabout, but in this instance, to help with the shoveling. I put my medical bag on the floor of the back seat. To it I'd added special items, such things as a powerful flashlight; sterile items such as gloves, forceps, scissors, and scalpel; two litres of saline for irrigations; an anesthetic – Pentothal; sterile tape; and an airway, just in case.

We crossed Charlottetown Harbour on the old wood-planked bridge and, once on the other side, we followed the main highway. By the time we reached Tea Hill, three miles out, we'd been stuck twice and had to shovel our way free. It didn't get any easier as we went on. The rising wind was whipping the snow into drifts and the farther we went, the bigger the drifts became. Sometimes the snow and wind caused complete white-outs, so we had to stop for minutes at a time until we could see again. On we crawled and shoveled – past Alexandra, past Cherry Valley. About six o'clock, we struggled into the country hotel at Vernon Bridge. We'd traveled fifteen miles in those six hours and felt as if we had shoveled the whole way. All of us were exhausted and hungry. It was impossible to go farther in this snowmobile.

I got directions for using the crank phone hanging on the wall in the tiny lobby and reached the operator. "This is Doctor Read."

"Oh," she said, "I'm so glad you've arrived at the hotel safely. We've been following you along. All the folks along the road have been calling in. They've been worried. I suppose you want to talk to the man in Roseberry. He's been trying to reach you."

"Well, yes, I do. Thanks a lot."

I was surprised by what the operator had said. I hadn't been on the Island long enough to learn that the telephone operators knew where everyone was and everything that was going on, what with the party line and all.

"How's your wife?" I asked when he came on the line.

"She's worse, Doc. She's crying from the pain and her temperature has gone up to 104." His voice was filled with alarm, even despair. I thought it was a little garbled and wondered if he'd been into the shine. "You gotta come. I'll pay you anything you ask, anything."

I realized that he was desperate, but that last part really annoyed me. I wasn't doing this for the money. I said with some heat, "Look, we've been six hours going fifteen miles and you're another thirteen or fourteen miles from here. The driver and his helper are both exhausted and I've done my share of shoveling, too. There's no way we can make it there by snowmobile, but I'm going to see if I can get a horse and sleigh. I'll do everything I can to help your wife."

"Thank God, Doc, you're one in a hundred and I'll reward you, you can be sure. When you get to Eldon, stop at the Putnams'. I'll have a fresh horse and driver waiting."

"Sir, I just said that I'll do my best to get there. In the meantime, don't let your wife have anything to eat, give her two aspirins, take the blankets off her, and sponge her with lukewarm water. I want her temperature down. Now repeat to me what I just said."

"Okay," he said, and repeated my directions, although haltingly. "I'll do anything you say. What about boiling some water?"

"Sure, go ahead," I said, smiling to myself. At least it was a way to keep him busy and, maybe, farther away from the bottle.

As soon as I hung up, the telephone rang with offers of assistance. The party line was at work. Everyone knew and wanted to help. Vernon Bruce, the village butcher, said he had to go to Orwell Cove and would be happy to take me along. "That's four miles and would be halfway to Eldon," he said. I immediately accepted, but wondered why anyone would go to Orwell Cove on a night like this.

I called Anne. "We're in Vernon River and everything is fine. A Mr. Bruce is going to take me in his sleigh on the next part of this journey. He's experienced, so don't worry."

"I do. Please be careful."

"Sure will."

While waiting for Bruce to arrive, we all had hot roast beef sandwiches, apple pie, and coffee, and then I began the next stage of my journey, the others hunkering down in the hotel for the night.

In the sleigh I was, of course, much more exposed to the storm than in the snowmobile. The snow was coming down even more heavily than before, the gale-force winds, having now shifted into the northwest, had freshened and the temperature had dropped even farther. Now I knew what a blizzard was. A poem about the Kee Bird that was said to live in the Arctic came into my mind, but all I could remember was the last line, "Kee Kee Krist but it's cold." My nose began to run. Bruce said, "When your nose turns blue and starts to run, we call it 'nosey' weather."

Seated in the sleigh behind Bruce, wrapped in my father's old coon coat and covered by a buffalo skin rug, I was just on the edge of feeling cold, but overall I was as comfortable as one can be with the sleigh jerking irregularly up and down and sideways. Driving on through the fierce blizzard, snow pelting in my face, I felt that this storm was simply an adversary we had to defeat. As time went on, I saw how skillfully Bruce was driving an unmarked country road at night, with drifts sometimes so high they reached the mare's belly. I admired Mr. Bruce's skill, how he controlled the sometimes plunging and temporarily frantic animal, and didn't once use his whip. How did he keep on track? What landmarks was he using? I hadn't seen anything but snow.

At the General Store in Orwell Cove, I talked briefly with Bruce. "I can't thank you enough for the ride. What a hell of a job you did! I don't know how you even knew whether you were on the road or how you knew where you were going. If I'm able to look after this woman, it'll be because of your coming out on a night like this."

"Oh," he said. "I'm glad I was able to help. We all

have to band together at times like these. But I must say, that's the worst night I've ever been out driving around in."

Much to my surprise, Johnny MacWilliams from Eldon was waiting there for me. "I had some supplies to get here and I was wondering how you were going to get to Eldon, so I thought I would just combine the two," he said. "I'm ready to leave now."

I couldn't see that he'd bought anything, so I assumed the party line had alerted him to my problem. Both Johnny and Bruce qualified as "salt of the earth" type of men, I decided.

This next four miles were much easier as the storm seemed to be rapidly petering out. The wind was not howling the way it had been and now I thought it wasn't snowing as hard and it seemed a bit warmer. We could even talk a bit. Johnny chatted away, telling me about his wife, Ruby, whom I knew professionally. "Todd Phillips, she's another patient of yours, is my sister. She and her two small children are staying with us in our family home. Her husband's in the US Navy and in a destroyer in the South Pacific." By the time we arrived in Eldon, I felt I knew all the goings-on in the village of Eldon.

The grandfather clock in the Putnams' parlour

when we arrived in Eldon showed it was ten-thirty. The next driver, Bill Black, was already there, waiting with his horse and sleigh and he had some welcome news. "I think the storm's all over. We should have a really nice ride to Roseberry."

After a few minutes' rest and some delicious bacon and eggs, toast, and coffee, we set off on our journey. "On to Roseberry," I felt like cheering as we left.

When we came to Annie's house we stopped, so I could let her know the current situation. When I told her about the most recent pleadings, she shook her head and said, "I wouldn't be trustin' that man. He's earned all the devils that haunt him from his bedposts. You never can tell how much truth there'd be in what he'd be saying."

Annie's comments bothered me, but after a moment I shrugged. "I guess I'll just have to deal with him as best I can. Now I have to look after his wife. But would you please give my Anne a call and tell her everything is okay."

Much to my surprise, Annie gave me a hug and, as I was leaving, said, "Be careful." She'd never been so demonstrative before.

The driver's forecast was correct. The four miles to Roseberry were like driving through a beautiful dream. The storm was over. The snow had stopped. The wind had completely died. Above, the full moon and the brightest stars I had ever seen made the snow-covered countryside seem as bright as day. On the road, the snow lay undisturbed. Except for the muffled klop-klop of the horse's hooves and the rhythmic jingle of the sleigh bells, the silence was crystal clear. The newly fallen snow covered everything. At the elegantly simple white church at Belfast, the gravestones had new white caps. So did the fence posts and the bridge railings and the snow on the spruce trees made them look like trees decorated for Christmas. Never had I experienced a more beautiful night.

And then it was over, for we had turned into the lane leading to the patient's house. Her husband greeted me with slightly slurred words, "Are you the Doc? You're even younger than I expected. How much experience have you had? Anyway, it's about time you got here."

It wasn't the kind of welcome I'd expected. I took a look at him – unshaven, hair unkempt, and breath smelling of alcohol.

After I peeled off my outside clothes and washed my hands thoroughly in the kitchen sink, I said,

"Now I'd like to examine your wife. Please take me to her."

He led me to a nearby bedroom where she was lying on a huge feather bed, covered only by a sheet. She attempted a welcoming smile, but it flickered. I noticed the pallour of her face and that her hair had not been tended to. There was no question in my mind but that this was one sick woman.

I pulled a chair to her bedside. "How are you feeling?"

"Not very good, Doctor. The pain's pretty bad and I feel so weak." I could barely hear her.

An older woman, who seemed quite calm and turned out to be her mother and a once-upon-a-time nurse, said, "Her temperature's down to 102F. I took off her blankets and sponged her, just as you said."

"Good for you." I was relieved that she seemed to have some savvy and didn't spend all her time talking. She would be useful.

I did a quick, but under the circumstances, reasonably thorough physical examination. There was no question about the diagnosis – multiple breast abscesses in her right breast, some cracks in her other nipple, but no other abnormalities. She had to be operated on. I felt my heart rate quicken and throat tighten.

Her husband had asked how much experience I'd had. I hadn't replied, and for good reason. I hadn't learned about this in medical school, nor had I ever seen or done the procedure I was about to undertake, either as a medical student or as an intern. But, happily, I remembered that one time when I was home for Christmas vacation, I'd gone with our family doctor to our local hospital and watched him do this very procedure. It hadn't looked very difficult. What a fortunate happenstance, I thought. What if I hadn't done that?

The best light was in the kitchen, but the kitchen table was too short and couldn't be extended, so I decided I'd have to do the operation in her bed. With her mother's help, I arranged three floor lights to get the best possible illumination. Her husband was the ever watchful observer, but said nothing. I noticed he seemed to be becoming more and more agitated. Was the smell of alcohol more prominent? I couldn't be sure. Finally he slumped down in a chair in the corner of the room. I heard him mutter, "Nothing better happen to my wife."

I glanced at him. Was he holding something in his lap? My heart began to beat faster and I felt beads of sweat break out on my forehead. The memory of a frightening experience one of my classmates had had in medical school flashed through my head. He, a student nurse, and an obstetrical resident had gone to deliver a woman on the third floor of a walk-up apartment in one of the poorer parts of Montreal. There, the husband was drunk and aggressive and had settled himself on a stool where he could watch everything they did. Just as they were about to deliver the baby, he yelled, "Nothing better happen to my wife or to the baby." The pistol he'd been holding in his lap and was then fingering reinforced his words. But, as my friend said, "We had a job to do and we forced ourselves to ignore him. Fortunately everything went well and we left unharmed but emotionally drained." Such memories do live on.

Just then my patient called out to her husband in a weak but surprisingly firm voice, "Why do you always have to be such a fool? Stop whatever you're doing. Be useful for once in your life. Go look after the baby. She probably needs changing. Do something – anything. Just get the hell out of here." Apparently she realized that her husband had done or said something that had interfered with my proceeding with the operation.

To my relief, he got up and left.

At last everything was set, and, with her mother holding the flashlight I'd brought, I put a tourniquet around the patient's arm. When I saw she had a large readily accessible vein, I felt better. A good omen. The needle went in the very first attempt. I checked it by withdrawing a little blood into the barrel of the syringe. It flowed easily. Good. Now for the Pentothal. I was very aware there was a risk of laryngeal spasm as I injected it, so I paused to make sure the airway I'd brought with me was within easy reach. As I had instructed her, she started to count slowly: one, two, three, four, five, six, -seven, --eight, ---nine. She didn't reach ten; she was asleep, breathing regularly without obstruction of the air passage. So far, so good.

I began to operate and all went smoothly. She awoke just as I finished. I checked her pulse, blood pressure, and respiratory rate; all were normal. I felt myself beginning to relax.

A few minutes later, as I was putting my equipment away, my patient reached over, took my hand, and brought it to her cheek. "Thank you," she murmured.

"You'll be fine now. You're a brave woman," I

replied, squeezing her hand gently. "I'll examine the baby before I leave and give your mother a new formula for her. Your mother was a great help; she's still a great nurse."

The baby was fine; her only problem, her grandmother said, was that she was a little constipated. "That's probably because she hasn't been getting enough fluids," I said. "But I'll give you a formula that has a little molasses in it, anyway. That should look after the constipation."

That done, I suddenly felt drained and had difficulty keeping my thoughts together. But I was sure there was something else I needed to do, but what was it? "Oh yes, I'll leave you enough of this new antibacterial, Sulfadiazine, to last ten days. Have your daughter take one tablet every six hours until they're all gone, together with lots of water."

Her husband, obviously less anxious, silently led us back to the sleigh.

Bill drove me back to Annie's. It was a little after three in the morning.

About noon the next day, Annie awakened me. "You had a call from your patient. She said to tell you she feels fine. Her temperature's normal and she's up and about as good as new. And oh, I called your wife this morning and told her you were fine and that you'd be home this evening."

Annie paused, then said, "Oh, I'm so relieved. I was so worried about you." She looked so happy. A big smile seemed to fill her whole face, and a few tears, which she quickly brushed away, completed the picture. She looked as proud as if I were her own son.

"Thanks for calling my wife, and thanks for all you've done for me."

Mid-afternoon Tim and Bill arrived in the snowmobile, having spent the night in Vernon River as planned. On our return trip to Charlottetown, we all felt very content. We had done what we started out to do, but we realized it was only because Vernon and MacWilliams had voluntarily gone out into that blizzard. We truly admired them for what they had done.

I had never sent a bill for my services. All of my patients either paid right away or came over to my office at Annie's within a few days and settled up. But in the more than four months since I operated and subsequently made four follow-up visits to her home, her husband had not showed up. I decided it was time for me to send them a bill.

I didn't have the foggiest idea how much to charge. I asked Annie what she thought. "He's a real skinflint and you can't be a trustin' him, but he's got the money. He's got a good farm and he does the lobster fishing when the season's open, so he's not poor. Imagine him not havin' paid for what you did, after all this time."

Finally I decided on seventy-five dollars. "Should be twice that much," Annie said, "what with the storm an' all." Some of the doctors in the city with whom I talked about the situation said it "should be five times that amount." Well, I decided, "better too little than too much."

Three days later I was in my office on the third floor when the Officer of the Day called me to say that a man wanted to see me and warned that he seemed very upset. I'd hardly put the phone down when he burst through the door, not having bothered to knock, red in the face and waving my recently sent statement. "What do you mean, sending me a huge bill like this? I thought you were somebody special, but I see you're just another money-grubbing doctor."

His voice was loud enough to be heard in Roseberry. Then he stomped across the room, threw the bill on my desk in front of me, and stood there, facing me, his hands on his hips, his eyes ablaze. He looked so belligerent I was glad my desk separated us.

I'm sure my mouth must have dropped open; I was so surprised by this turn of events. Was this the same man who had pleaded for me to go twenty-eight miles in a blinding snowstorm and who said he'd pay me anything? For what must have been a minute or so I sat as if transfixed. I couldn't believe this. That there were people like this, I already knew, but I didn't expect to find one in an idyllic community like this one. Now I knew what Annie was warning me about. Knowing it made me feel I now shared in the secrets of the district. No longer was I an outsider, I belonged.

I'd studied medicine because I thought it would be intellectually and scientifically interesting, but especially because I'd be able to help people; helping people was in my family's tradition. It seemed to me that so far I'd been true to my concept of what being a physician was all about. Now this man was trying to reduce it all to dollars and cents. Well, he wasn't going to succeed.

I picked up the bill, methodically tore it into pieces and dropped them into the wastebasket. When I spoke I heard my voice as it had never sounded before; it was dripping with disdain. "You don't owe me a cent. I've already been well paid by all the wonderful experiences I had in going to your wife and that she's alive and well."

The colour drained from his face and his shoulders drooped. He looked confused, embarrassed, deflated. It seemed he didn't know what to say or do. I felt very calm as I got up from my chair, walked to the door, opened it, and said to my assistant, "This man is leaving. Please show him out."

Then I walked over to the window. Bathed by the warm May sun, the scene below was far distant from the swirling blizzard back in January. My thoughts went back to how hard Tim and his helper and I had worked during the snowmobile drive to Vernon River, how all the people along our route had kept track of us and told the operator so help always would have been near, how the skill and fortitude of Bruce and MacWilliams guiding horse and sleigh through a blinding blizzard allowed us to reach Eldon, how much I'd enjoyed the moonlit dazzling beauty of the sleigh ride from Eldon, how relieved and satisfied I felt for having successfully operated on my patient and how grateful she had been, and how much Annie's warmth and support had meant to me.

I fully realized I had been fortunate to have had this experience, one that was possible only because of the support of all these people. This man's meanness only served to accentuate the richness of what all the others had done. I was grateful.

CHAPTER EIGHT

Amongst the most memorable characters in my practice were Ed and Mary Harrington who lived in a small house almost opposite Annie's. They looked after the properties of the Putnams who were usually away. This included the cows and hens; what else I never knew. Oftentimes I would drop in to see them just because it was enjoyable and they always seemed to be so glad to see me. I thought of them as being real people. They were as they were, nothing fancy, no pretenses.

Once a month when my new supply of scripts

arrived, I made a special call on them, so much so that it became almost a ritual. I would say, "Annie told me you both are a bit under the weather, so I thought I'd better make a professional visit." And then after checking them both over, "Now I can see that both of you really do need some medicine." Then I'd give each of them a script.

I don't know whether they considered it a *quid pro quo* or not, but every week I bought from them, at a very low price, a pint of cream and a dozen eggs. When my wife opened the packages when I got home, she always found nineteen or twenty eggs and cream so thick she had to spoon it out of the jar.

One time when I was sitting in the wardroom, I began thinking about my relationship with Ed and Mary, and this led me to think about the various relationships I'd had with my patients during my time in the navy, and realized that these relationships had varied depending on the circumstances. I thought of what I'd done in emergencies; I'd been active and my patient passive. I'd done whatever needed to be done to try to save the patient's life – I didn't even ask permission. That seemed appropriate, I thought.

But it was different when a patient came to me with, for example, a sore throat. Then I'd done those things necessary to make a diagnosis: taken a history, done a physical examination, and enough laboratory tests to be sure enough of the diagnosis so that I knew how to treat the patient; I explained what the treatment was and details of how often, etc. This I did by saying, "*I want you* to take this medicine in the way I just described," much like the way a loving parent would speak to a child. I decided never to use the words "should" or "ought" because I personally always reacted negatively to these words. It seemed to me that using those words would result in patients or children doing the opposite or cause anger or rebellion. The last thing I wanted was an angry patient or child. Those words I classified as being angry parent words. That contrasted with the caring parent words of "I want you to – ."

Driving home one night after talking with Ed and Mary, I began thinking about the relationship of doctors to patients with ongoing diseases, for example, diabetes. In this situation the doctor would have taught the patient how to treat the patient's disease, using insulin and an appropriate diet, for example, as a caring parent would teach a child. But, subsequently, the relationship would change to one in which there were two individuals discussing a mutually interesting subject. While the doctor would inform the patient of new developments in treatments and such, the patient would tell the doctor of any concerns and ask for suggestions. This would no longer be a parent-child relationship, but adult-adult. I decided I'd have to explore these ideas more fully in the future.

CHAPTER NINE

Throughout the winter, I had continued making my twice-weekly visits by snowmobile to Annie's front parlour and to look after the usually small number of patients who came to see me. But on March 28, the end of that season was clearly signaled. On this day there was not a cloud in the sky and the sun took full advantage. From the time it rose to the time it set, it poured its radiant heat on the land below. Even before lunch, the snowbanks were shrinking. Rivulets from the melting snow began to fill the ditches and make ever-expanding puddles. Soon, these puddles and slush covered the sidewalks and streets of Charlottetown and made wearing overshoes an absolute, but not always adequate, necessity. Although the temperature was only in the forties, the warmth of the sun clearly said spring was on its way.

Shortly after lunch, Tim Ryan called me on the phone, his Texan accent unmistakable. "It doesn't look as if we're going to have to shovel any snow today, Doc, so I'm leaving Bill home. He's got some things he has to catch up on anyway. I'll be along shortly. Is that okay with you?"

"Sure," I said. "Should be a great day for a ride in the country. I'll be ready whenever you get here."

In about half an hour, Tim arrived with the snow-mobile. He'd been a Mobil Oil Company employee in various parts of the world for some twenty years. I, having worked with him for the past few months, fully understood why. He was not given to a lot of talk and he'd never told me much about himself, but I'd quickly developed confidence in him because he'd demonstrated he was reliable and knew what he was doing. I guess that Mobil shared the same opinion and that's why they'd put him in charge of the oil well the company was drilling offshore in Charlotte-town Harbour in Hillsborough Bay.

We followed our usual routine that day, crossing the half-mile-wide Charlottetown Harbour on the ice, thus avoiding a very uncomfortable ride crossing the old wooden bridge. In Eldon I found that, for some reason – maybe the spring-like weather – an unusually large number of patients were waiting to see me, and they kept coming all afternoon. Their complaints seemed to be those they'd probably accumulated all winter. I began to wonder if many simply wanted an excuse to get out and about in the warmth of the day, or perhaps to see or talk to a person they'd not been looking at all winter. Failing to find many significant abnormalities, I did my best to satisfy them by listening intently to whatever they had to say and to respond in what I thought to be an appropriate way. Having done all this, I made sure they all got a new supply of multivitamin tablets. I'd long since learned that "the laying on of hands" – at least mine – was not enough.

By the time we'd finished dinner and were ready to start for home, it was already dark. A telephone lineman by the name of Bob asked if he could ride back with us. Of course we said okay, and he got in the back seat where I sat when Bill was with us. After going only a short distance, we saw that the sun had melted much of the snow on the highway, so for long stretches the gravel was exposed.

Tim said, "Driving like this all twenty-odd miles to Charlottetown is going to be very difficult, take a long time, and it's not going to do the snowmobile any good. What d'ya say we go down to the shore here at Lower Newton and go back on the ice across Hillsborough Bay?"

That appealed to me, so I said, "Sounds like the better way to go. It'd be a lot shorter, too. Shouldn't be more than about ten or twelve miles, 'cause we could go straight across to Tea Hill. And you were out to Governor's Island earlier this morning and the ice was good, you said."

"Yup, it was good, no problems."

We got on the ice near Lower Newton, then skirted McInnis Point and went straight towards Tea Hill. Ordinarily, I felt anxious when we were driving on ice, even though in the past few months I'd watched horse races on the frozen surface of Charlottetown Harbour, as well as cars crossing the North River on the ice. This evening I was less concerned than usual as we skimmed across the smooth ice of Hillsborough Bay. Perhaps it was because I knew Tim was both a careful and experienced driver on ice, as every day all winter he'd driven on ice to the oilrig on Governor's Island. Or perhaps it was because it was because this time I was sitting in the front seat, from where I could more easily get out than if I first had to climb over the front seat, especially as I was wearing a bulky raccoon coat. Knowing how uncomfortable and how long the trip home would have been had we stayed on the highway also made me more readily accept whatever the risks of this ice travel might be.

Even so, I was relieved when after some time we regained the shore at Tea Hill. As we expected, that highway was also bare. We again tried driving with one ski and track on the highway and the other ski and track on the still snow-covered shoulder. The going during these three miles was slow and difficult, so when we reached the near shore of the Harbour, we decided to abandon the road and cross on the ice as we had earlier in the day.

The scene was entirely different than when we'd crossed the Harbour on our way to Eldon. That seemed a very short time ago, but then the ice was illuminated by brilliant sunshine. Now it was our headlights that pierced the darkness of the night and illuminated the whiteness of the ice road that lay before us. The only other light came from the sparkle of the lights on the buildings and streets of Charlottetown on the opposite shore. Just another half-mile and we'd be there.

As we began this last stage of our journey on the ice road, I noticed that Tim drove much more slowly than he had when crossing the bay. Very smart, because about halfway across I saw that not far ahead our white road disappeared. I didn't have to be told what that meant – open water. I felt Tim jam on the brakes, but I wasn't sure we were going to stop in time. The blackness came closer. I decided I'd better get ready to get out while we were still on ice and I opened the door beside me a little and positioned myself to get out quickly. Finally we stopped, just in time. Another three or four feet and we'd have been in the water.

Even as we stopped, I felt the snowmobile begin to break through the rotting ice. I pushed the door the rest of the way open and slid out, face down on the ice. As I did, I thought I saw Tim doing the same on the driver's side. Still lying prone, I turned around. Already the snowmobile had sunk to where water covered the floorboards.

I looked for Bob. There he was, trying to climb

over the back of the front seat and seemed to be unable to move any further. In a flash I realized that had Bill been with us, that would have been me. Bob screamed, "Doc, I'm stuck, I can't get out. Help!" I edged closer to the edge of the ice and was able to grab his hand. I pulled; he didn't budge. I felt sweat break out on my forehead. I wiggled as close to the edge of the ice as I dared. The snowmobile had sunk even lower. It was now or never. This time I managed to get a grip around his wrist; he did the same with mine. I took a deep breath and pulled with all my might, my strength probably magnified by my desperation. To my relief, he came out and lay on the ice beside me, breathing rapidly. Was I relieved!

"Let's get farther away from the edge. Right now!" I shouted in his ear, as he seemed in a trance-like state. He roused himself enough to crawl beside me away from the water. Then I got him to his feet and we walked about ten feet back towards the shore where the ice seemed quite solid. Tim soon joined us and the three us watched the last minutes of our snowmobile. It went down tail first, its headlights turning the water a blue-green until they went out and there was nothing but a black hole. With it went the ice that Bob and I had so recently been lying on.

Memories of the sinking of the destroyer *Bickerton* in the Arctic the previous August flooded my mind. It had gone down stern first, too. That time there was no darkness. This time there were no casualties. Not so far, anyway.

My eyes had quickly adapted to the dark so I was able to see how my companions looked. Bob's mouth was open, showing his lower teeth: his forehead was furrowed and his eyes were wide open. All this meant to me that he was scared. "We're going to drown," he gasped.

"Nonsense," I said. "None of us are going to drown if we keep our wits about us." I wasn't surprised that he paid no attention to what I'd just said.

As I expected, Tim seemed in total control of himself. Shortly after the snowmobile's lights went out, he said, very calmly, "I believe we're in a heap of trouble. What do you think we should do?"

I seemed to have the same state of total mental and physical alertness that I'd experienced the previous August when our aircraft carrier, *Nabob*, was torpedoed. My mind and my body felt totally mobilized, ready to deal with the predicament we were facing. But this time was different. That time I just had to get to my action stations; this time I realized that these men were here because of me. They were my responsibility. It was up to me to get them to safety.

We were standing on ice that I thought was about to break up and float out the Harbour. Being as dark as it was, it seemed to me a long shot that anyone knew we were out here. No one was going to come and rescue us. We were on our own. The problem was for us – for me – to solve.

Bob said, "We should stay right here till morning. Then someone is sure to see us and come to get us."

"Yeah," Tim responded, "and they can get a boat and pick us up from a cake of ice out in Hillsborough Bay. Fat chance they'd find us."

Obviously the idea of waiting for a rescue didn't appeal to Tim, nor did it to me. I was well aware how quickly the ice could break up once it started. We had to get off this ice as fast as we could.

Realizing this, I said, "Look, you guys, we can't stay here waiting for someone to save us, because I don't think anyone knows we're here. The ice is going to break up and it can go damn fast. We've got to get moving, right now. I think we're more than halfway across, so we might as well see if we can go the rest of the way. If we find we can't make it in that direction, we'll turn around and go back to where we got on the ice. I don't want to go that way if we can help it. It's a long distance from the landfall to the bridge, and crossing it is a good hike all by itself. I don't want to make that walk tonight, if I can help it. Are you with me?"

Tim said, "Let's go." Bob nodded.

Both of them having agreed, I continued. "I weigh a lot less than either of you two guys, and as these flying boots I'm wearing help spread my weight, I'll lead the way. You two follow in single file. Bob, you stay about ten feet behind me. Tim, stay about the same distance behind Bob. You got that?"

I paused for a moment to allow them to respond. Neither said anything, but they looked as if they understood. I went on, "If I go through the ice, for God's sake, don't try to rescue me or all of us will go. Just turn around and go back to the other shore, as best you can. Now remember, you're going to follow exactly in my tracks. Okay?"

I figured we were already more than halfway across. That meant we had, at worst, not more than about four hundred yards to go. Not very far, but it seemed like a formidable distance. I noticed that the ice cap up near the bridge looked as if it was still intact, so I decided that was the direction to start in. After about a couple hundred paces, I would begin looking for a way to make the crossing.

I said, "Okay, let's go," and started walking toward the bridge. I was very careful, putting one foot down at a time and making sure my footing was solid before trusting it with my full weight. Even so, I hadn't gone fifty feet before my left foot broke through ice that looked solid, but turned out to be little more than shell ice that I hadn't seen. Before I knew it, ice-cold water was pouring in over the top of my boot. There I was, one foot below the ice, my weight on my outstretched hands and my right knee. Fortunately, it didn't take long to extricate myself from this position and empty the freezing water from my boot. From then on, I was even more careful than before.

What really prolonged our journey were patches of open water, which would suddenly open up, often just ahead of us. They were disconcerting, as well as forcing us to find a way around each one of them. That took precious time. At one point a loud cracking sound signaled that a three-foot stretch of water had opened just behind Tim, separating us from the ice on the shore from which we'd started. Now we had no choice but to go forward; there was no way back. Little by little we edged forward, but often it seemed a case of "two feet forward, one foot back." It was hard to keep from being discouraged.

When we were no more than about a hundred feet from the shore, I sensed the ice was becoming increasingly unstable, as if it were floating free, no longer attached to the shore. Fearing it would totally break away at any moment and start floating away with us on it, I shouted, "This is it, men. Run like hell for the shore!"

I'm sure none of us had ever run so fast with as much purpose. The ice pack had pulled away from the shore so that we had to jump the last couple of feet. We made it and stood on the shore, panting. Our flight had not been a minute too soon. Already the Harbour scene had changed; no longer was it as it had been just a few minutes before. The ice pack had broken in ragged fragments, often piling up on top of one another, only to slip off and go crashing into the water. Carried by a brisk current, the ice had started on its journey to oblivion.

"Jeez," Bob said. "Do I need a drink!"

He wasn't the only one.

CHAPTER TEN

On one of those lovely days that occur only when spring is blossoming on Prince Edward Island, I was driving to Orwell Cove to see a patient when my panel truck came to a sudden stop. I revved the motor. The vehicle would go neither forward nor backward. I got out to see what kind of trouble I was in. That didn't take long. Spring had arrived and the frost was leaving the secondary roads. All four wheels had sunk to their axles in the wet red clay. There was no digging a way out of this. Towing was the only answer. I needed help. Looking around, I saw a farmer with a team of horses on a nearby hill. I waved.

He understood and soon was with me. "Hi, Doc. I'm Jim MacPherson. Looks like you need some help."

"Sure do. I'm lucky to have you up on that hill, just waiting for me, of course. But these horses of yours, I'm impressed. Clydesdales, aren't they?"

"Yep. Best I've ever had. Sometimes I just take them out of the barn and look at them, a matched pair of chestnut-coloured Clydesdales. I never thought I'd ever have such a beautiful team."

I looked them over carefully, not knowing anything about horses. They looked as if they were at least six feet tall and had elegant heads with a straight profile, large dark eyes, a heavy forelock, and long necks. The muscles in their shoulders and hindquarters were remarkable, I thought. And then I noticed the long hairs that fell from just below the knees and covered their white hooves that were about to be covered with mud.

"Such extraordinary horses," I said to Jim. "You must be very proud of them."

"And wait till you see them work – they are extraordinarily energetic."

He hitched them to my panel truck with a stout chain and they bent to the task of freeing it from the mud. Not a problem. My vehicle was free.

I offered to pay. He refused. But then I pulled out my magic booklet and extracted a script. Would he accept one of these? You betcha – with enthusiasm.

This same scene recurred several times over the next ten days, sometimes with horses (no more matched Clydesdales), but more often a tractor. Wonderful items to have in one's pocket, those scripts.

CHAPTER ELEVEN

It turned out that the diagnosis of the next patient puzzled me for fifty years.

When I arrived at my office one day in mid-April, Annie met me at the door. Without even saying hello, she said, "The Goodys called a bit ago and said they would like you to come see their ten-year-old daughter, Polly. She has some big painful lumps on her legs and they're itchy, too. You don't have any patients waiting, so you could go right now."

Over the past seven months I'd come to know this Annie McRae as one remarkable woman. She'd treated me not as a landlady but as if I were her son, always worrying because of my being thin and almost demanding I stay and have dinner with her before returning home. She seemed to know everybody and all the "goings-on" in the entire district. I realized she was now telling me not only to get on my way, but also that the family only asked for help when they believed they really needed it.

"They're really nice folks. They don't have much money, but they're proud and they're not about accepting charity," Annie said. "They have a small farm and he also does the lobster fishing. He's doing it now, 'cause in this part of Prince Edward Island the season is only open between the middle of April and the end of June. They eat lobster for breakfast, dinner, and supper. Even if you like lobster, it must be really tiresome to have it for every meal. With the cold'n'all in the early morning hours when they go out to their traps, it's a hard way to make a livin'."

Her comments reminded me that I'd already had some inkling of how hard lobster fishermen work. I'd gone out and worked with them once at five o'clock in the morning while I was still in my teens. But that was in late June, a totally different scene. I shuddered when I thought what it would be like under the variety of weather conditions that occur in the spring: freezing temperatures and winds, sometimes even gales.

Rumours were prevalent that lobsters were unusually scarce this spring; it was not a rumour that the fishermen were only getting twenty-five cents a pound. To add to their difficulties, about ten days earlier a vicious spring storm ripped a large number of traps loose from their moorings. I'd seen them on the shore where they lay twisted, damaged beyond repair and usually partially buried in the sand. I knew how much such losses added to the fishermen's costs.

I was concerned because I had quite a number of lobster fishermen and their families as patients. But now I wanted to see this young girl and get back to my office as quickly as I could. So I said, "Annie, tell me exactly where they live."

"They live in Pinette," she said. "That's about three miles down the highway to the Wood Islands Ferry. You'll see a small white house on the left side of the road just before you get to the bridge. It's all by itself. You won't be a missin' it."

I didn't, for it was just as Annie had described it. I turned into their lane. On its right-hand side stood a slightly raised wooden platform, which I assumed was where lobster traps were stored the nine-and-a-half months they were not in use. On the left side, between the house and the road, a good-sized vegetable garden had already been partially prepared for planting. In the yard in front of the house, I noticed a Model A Ford and several pieces of well-used farm machinery scattered haphazardly. Behind the house, a huge pile of firewood largely hid an outdoor privy, a quarter-moon cut into the door. The house looked bigger than it had from the highway, its major features being an outside red brick chimney, vertically placed board and batten, steeply pitched roof, a wide verandah running the width of the house, and a centrally placed front door. From a cursory inspection, I couldn't be sure whether the house was painted white or whitewashed.

I knocked on the front door. A woman, whom I judged to be in her late thirties, opened it. "You must be the doctor," she said. "I've been watching for you."

"Yes, I'm Doctor Read," thinking it must be pretty obvious, as there were not too many men hereabouts wearing a naval officer's uniform with red and gold stripes on their sleeves. I thought everyone must know I was still in the navy.

"Do come in. I'm Annette, Polly's mother," she said, as she led me to the living room, located immediately to the left of the vestibule. Of average size, it was sparsely but adequately furnished. Grouped around the fireplace, where a rock maple log was burning, were a sofa and several chairs, all well-worn. She apparently thought she should tell me why she had a fire in it when the outside temperature was quite warm. "For the past few weeks our furnace has been broken and we can't afford to get it fixed just now, so we've kept a fire in the fireplace almost continuously. Even when the day is quite comfortable outside, it's still damp and chilly in here, and the temperature drops come evening…

"Let me show you how I warm up," she said, and walked over to the fireplace, turned her back to it and lifted up the back of her skirt high enough so she exposed her backside to the heat, yet not visible to me. "I wouldn't do this, except you're a doctor and I think you need to know everything about how we live."

Even so, she looked a little embarrassed. She didn't need to be. I'd seen my mother do the same thing many times when I was growing up and had either thought nothing of it or saw it as being funny. I later learned that in Scotland where women often used this method of warming up, it was called "central heating," or sometimes "heating your Ayrshire" (the emphasis being on the "r"). I nodded and smiled. "That should warm you up. Does Polly do that, too?"

"Oh no, she doesn't approve of it. But quite often recently, she stands facing the fire and pulls her skirt up, but only to her knees. I'll go get her. She's in her bedroom."

She soon returned with a slender young girl. I thought she looked about the average height for a nine- or ten-year-old girl, a little pale and quite thin. Neat and clean, her pink flannelette nightgown covered her from the neck down. Her long brown hair looked as if she had recently brushed it and tied it in a ponytail. A shy smile illuminated her face.

I rose to meet her and, shaking her hand, said, "I hear you've been having some problems. Do have a seat on the sofa and tell me about what's troubling you." I pulled a chair near her. "Your mother told me you have some sore places on your legs."

She nodded and pulled up her nightgown, exposing her legs to just beyond her knees. On both shins, I saw four or five raised lumps. All were similar, about an inch to an inch-and-a-half in diameter, red and purple in colour, the centre raised about a quarter-inch. They were warm and she winced when I touched them. None of them were fluctuant, indicating there was no underlying fluid, such as pus.

Suddenly she blurted out, "Doctor, they hurt all the time and they're so itchy it's hard not to scratch. I've been taking aspirin and that helps, but I've had them for over a week now. Please help me, Doctor."

The strength of her voice surprised me. "I'll do my best, Polly, but I do need to look at the rest of you, okay?"

She nodded, so I turned to her mother, "May I have a sheet or a blanket please, so I can examine her?"

With her mother's help, I did, from head to toe. She had no fever and her blood pressure and pulse were normal. Because she was so thin I wanted to be reasonably sure she didn't have tuberculosis in addition to her leg complaints, so I paid special attention to her lungs. They were clear. The only abnormalities were the lesions on her legs and some accompanying scratch marks.

I spent some time inquiring about her diet. "No, I've always had enough to eat. I've never gone to bed hungry." From a nutritional point of view, her diet also seemed adequate, although limited in variety and possibly a little low in Vitamin C.

I pursued the question with her mother. She, too, denied any problem related to quality and amount of food. "The only thing is that during the lobster season each spring we do eat a lot of lobster. That's the cheapest food we can get and sometimes we have it for breakfast, dinner, and supper. I must say, it does get a bit tiresome. But we survive." A wry smile flitted across her face.

After a pause, she went on. "School lunches are sometimes a problem, though. Polly and the other girls whose fathers are lobster fishermen really don't like taking lobster sandwiches to school. They think it shows that we're poor and they're ashamed of that. So, to hide it, they trade their lobster sandwiches with the kids who've brought peanut butter and jelly ones."

Although I had taken an unusually thorough history and done a very careful physical examination, I had to say, "I don't know what's causing Polly's problems nor what to do about it other than to continue with the aspirin when needed. But as soon as I get back to Charlottetown, I'll talk to Dr. Seaman and

Dr. MacKenzie and the two Dr.'s McMillan; they're the most knowledgeable doctors around here. I'll also see if I can find anything in the medical library at the Prince Edward Island Hospital. If I learn anything, I'll give you a call. In any case, I don't think it's anything serious and I'll be back to see Polly on Saturday."

As I expected, both mother and daughter looked disappointed, saying only, "Thanks for coming to see us, Doctor. We'll be hoping you find out something in Charlottetown."

The next two days I did my best to discover what was wrong with Polly. I found nothing in the library and none of the doctors had ever seen lesions like Polly's. One doctor, who was very interested in allergies, suggested that maybe she was allergic to something in her environment and offered me the loan of his testing equipment. I accepted. I'd never used these tests before but I knew enough about them that was sure I could do them without difficulty.

I administered the allergy tests, but none showed a positive reaction. However, I thought her lesions looked better and she said they were not as painful.

I again went back to see her the next Saturday. This time Polly's father was there, too, a tall lean man, dressed in worn but clean and mended over-alls, a heavy woolen grey sweater, and a battered fisherman's peaked cap. His weather-beaten face, piercing blue eyes, sinewy arms, and the rough skin of his hands were in keeping with the life he led. The thinness of his lips suggested he was a man of few words.

I noticed they didn't have a fire burning in the fireplace. "Oh, no," Polly's mother said. "We haven't had one since you were last here, the weather's been so warm."

Polly chimed in. "I feel so much better. I'm going back to school on Monday."

I looked at her legs. The lesions were smaller and the colour had almost disappeared. When I felt them, they were no longer hot or tender. I still didn't know the diagnosis, but the important thing was she was getting better.

Polly's father had not said a word since I first met him, but now he spoke up. "We appreciate all the attention you've paid to Polly, Doctor. My wife says you've been very thorough and understanding. Now we want to pay you for your services. How much do we owe you?"

I really didn't want to charge them anything

because I thought I hadn't done very much. But I remembered that Annie had said that they were people who did not want to accept charity. I felt I had to give them a bill. "I made four trips here from my office, so that makes twelve dollars," I said.

"Do you mind being paid in lobsters?"

"Of course not. That'll be fine."

With that I said good-bye to Polly and her mother and we went out to his truck, an ancient Ford half-ton, parked quite near the door. There he got a scale from the front seat, climbed up on the bed, and lifted the lid of a leather-hinged slatted wood box. It measured about two feet by four and had big Gs painted in red on its top and side. From it, he picked up the lobsters by their carapace, weighed each one, and put them in a large cardboard box. They were the liveliest lobsters I'd ever seen, their feelers waving wildly, and their claws reaching out in all directions for whatever they could grab for they were not banded. At thirty-six pounds, I said, "That's enough. It's even more than enough."

(I knew that at the going rate of twenty-five cents a pound, my fee demanded forty-eight pounds of lobster. But what would we do with that much lobster? Even thirty-six pounds was more than enough.)

"Are you sure?"

"Yes, I'm more than sure."

Before I got home it was almost ten. My wife and I decided that it was too late to cook them that night, so we left them crawling around in our back porch overnight. In the morning we boiled them in sea water, and that evening spread them out on our dining room table and invited our neighbours to eat their fill. Everyone agreed they were delicious. But as I dipped a luscious claw into a dish of melted butter, I thought not only about how much more medical knowledge I needed to learn, but also how much I'd learned about living from my patients.

In December of 2000 when I described the details of the case to my good friend, Dr. Jerry Solomons, who, like me, was an Emeritus Professor of Pediatrics of the University of Iowa College of Medicine, I finally got my answer. I knew he'd grown up in Glasgow, Scotland. "In winter," he said, "we often had damp and chilly weather. Not many people had central heating, so almost everybody depended on stoves and especially fireplaces for heating. We used to sit in a semi-circle, getting our hands and other parts as close to the heat as possible. Lesions, just as you describe, were common; red, sometimes purple, sometimes with white areas in the centre. There were many variations. Very common."

It was from that talk with Dr. Solomons that I finally knew the diagnosis. Chilblains.

CHAPTER TWELVE

In the spring of 1945, the problems with prohibition again boiled to the surface. The premier was Walter Jones, a great bull of a man who was known to often take drastic actions. The prohibitionists well knew that he owned a prize bull called "Moonshine" and strongly suspected he supported a liberalization of the Prohibition Act. They took every opportunity to remind him about what had happened to the Tories back in 1927. But he was also receiving letters from a veterans group, the Royal Canadian Legion, and others who strongly supported modernizing the act. Finally, in April, he introduced the Cullen

Amendment. This amendment to the Prohibition Act would mean prescriptions for liquor would be good for six months at a time. It passed with bipartisan support.

This new development occurred shortly before the annual meeting of the Prince Edward Island Medical Society. The doctors were "up in arms," the newspapers proclaimed. They said they would have nothing to do with the new scripts. It was time for "us to be rid of our unwanted role in the control of liquor" and they prepared a motion to be presented at their meeting.

The day before the Medical Association was to meet, I received my quota of the new scripts for both my navy and my private practice. They were identical to the old ones except that they stated they were valid for repeated use over six months. I put mine aside, anticipating what the other doctors would do and that I would never use them. But I also realized this would cause a major problem for the legislators. I wondered what would happen.

About ten o'clock the next morning, Carl came rushing up the stairs and into my office. As soon as he caught his breath, he said, "There's a huge queue that starts in front of the Revere Hotel near Queen

Street that goes up Kent all the way to the Avenue, over to Grafton and then back towards Queen as far as the Bank of Montreal."

"Why, that just about circles the whole of downtown," I exclaimed. "Did you find out why?"

"Well, I talked to several people and all of them had the same story. They said that everyone knew that the doctors had said they were not going to have anything to do with the new scripts. So when they heard about this one doctor – that's the one who's been selling the old ones for a living – selling the new ones, they all wanted to get one. One man, who'd bought one, said the doctor's room was on the third floor of the hotel. The queue started there and went down two flights of stairs and out the front door of the hotel. The doctor was sitting up in the bed in his pajamas. On the floor beside him was a big waste basket. You gave him ten bucks. He gave you a signed script. He tossed the ten bucks into the basket. As simple as that.

Once it was evident that at least one doctor was going to make the new scripts available, the doctors decided there was no point introducing their proposed motion.

"Carl, do you think that the premier masterminded the whole thing?" Certainly the news that this one doctor was selling the new scripts got around very quickly.

But this did not end the story. When the amendment to the act was laid before the Lieutenant Governor, he refused to sign it. Consequently it could not become law. That didn't faze Premier Jones. He continued to have the new scripts sent to the doctors and they were honoured in the government-owned vendors. As soon as the Lieutenant Governor's term expired, the premier appointed a new one. The new man signed the bill. But even this did not solve the problem because the question then arose whether this action was legal.

Several more years passed before the Legislature decreed the end of prohibition and scripts finally disappeared.

CHAPTER THIRTEEN

The months of June and July 1945 passed quickly. The war against Nazi Germany had been won. The war in the Pacific seemed to be quickly heading to the invasion of Japan, which was expected to be hard and difficult, with many casualties. Then came the Atom Bomb with its devastation of Hiroshima and Nagasaki, followed by the Japanese surrender. That was a day for celebration, especially in view of the probable saving of lives of at least a million Japanese and American soldiers.

Soon after this I learned that the people in my Eldon district had been successful in getting a full-time physician, so that I no longer needed to make my twice-a-week trips to my office in Annie's front parlour. That had been a great experience, but I was quite happy to call an end to those trips. More importantly, my wife Anne had become pregnant with a due date the following March. I felt I'd had an extraordinary experience in the navy, both on sea and on land, and I was able to obtain a residency in Paediatrics at the Children's Memorial Hospital (now The Montreal Children's Hospital) in Montreal, beginning the following July. Soon after, I obtained my discharge from the navy for early January 1946. With these preparations for my future in place, it was time to move on.

CHAPTER FOURTEEN

By 1961 my life as a country doctor on Prince Edward Island was long over, but my life as a vacationer there was in its infancy, for I had become so attached to the way of life on the Island that I was to return for a month almost every summer for the next thirty years. The first time I was back, I immediately wanted to renew my relationship with Emmett Robinson, whom I'd gotten to know in my last few weeks at HMCS Queen Charlotte. What I knew of his activities in the navy had intrigued me – a half-told story.

So it was that on Friday, July 10, 1961, having been on the Island for only a day, I was already on the wharf at Covehead on the north side of the Island, waiting for Emmett. When I'd talked to him on the phone soon after I arrived, he seemed to be pleased to hear from me and said, "Let's meet tomorrow at about six on the jetty. I've got a new boat and I'll take you for a ride in her. I'll show you what a beauty she is. And ya' know, if we're lucky, we might even find a few lobsters." Remembering Emmett's reputation, I sensed it could even become an adventure.

Sixteen years previously, in 1945. I'd first met him when he'd returned to the naval base, HMCS Queen Charlotte, in Charlottetown, Prince Edward Island, to get his honourable discharge. I was the Medical Officer.

Emmett was a sailor I still remembered vividly, probably because of his devil-may-care attitude. But more than that, I seemed to know him really well from the first moment I saw him, as if we'd been together in some earlier life. I was not surprised to learn that in his six years in the navy, he'd been in "Short Boats," the name the Brits had for their type of motor torpedo boats and used for frequent action-filled forays along the German-held coast of France. Nor was I surprised to learn that on that disastrous day when the German battleships, the *Scharnhorst* and *Gneisenau*, escaped the watching eyes of the Royal Navy and moved north through the English Channel, his craft was heavily engaged. When their gunner was killed, Emmett manned the Oerlikon machine gun and shot down a German aircraft, saving his boat. For this he was awarded a "gong," which he never put up, saying that things like ribbons were too showy. I'd always felt that he wouldn't be afraid of the devil itself.

I always wondered, but rarely asked him, about his wartime experiences – and he rarely mentioned them. What Emmett did enjoy talking about was the pleasure he'd had looting captured German ships in the Scheldte river that flows past Antwerp – not big stuff, just cigarettes and liquor and other such things – and sharing it with the Dutch population, newly liberated by the Canadian army. It seemed right in character; I often thought he would have made a great pirate.

One time he hinted that before the war he'd been involved in bootlegging here on the north shore of the Island. Although that was illegal, the people didn't consider it immoral. The service rendered by the smugglers was perceived as essential, but, more than that, the whole matter was looked upon as a kind of benign melodrama, played out by the rum-runners and the Mounties, complete with high-speed chases across dust-choked back roads, false landings, and road traps.

While waiting for Emmett to arrive, I surveyed the scene on and around the jetty. The lobster-fishing season had ended just a few days before. Stacks of lobster traps now were piled in more or less neat rows and brightly painted buoys and grizzled ropes lay haphazardly around them. The highway bridge and massive dunes of buff sand partially hid the mouth of the harbour. On the far side of the harbour, near the highway, somebody had left a small boat on a trailer. I guessed the owners had gone somewhere for dinner as I couldn't see a car parked there. Out on a sand bar, directly across from the jetty, what appeared to be a family – two adults and three children – were digging for clams. To my left, the harbour widened out to a bay. Three sailboats lay becalmed, their sails limp. I presumed they were tourists, for anyone fa-miliar with the area would have anticipated the late afternoon disappearance of the sea breeze. They were probably staying at the Stanhope Beach Inn. I looked up the near shore at the old summer hotel, sitting high on its red sandstone bluff, simple and stark in its newly washed clapboards and green painted shutters. Not even a tree protected this proud symbol of earlier days. I wondered how far away it was – maybe a half-mile. By road it was a good mile.

A slow-moving fishing boat passed by. I watched as the men caught a mooring buoy thirty or forty metres upstream, tied up, brought their dory alongside and rowed to shore. One of them carried a hemp bag, partially filled. I wondered what was in it. Mackerel had not started to run and the lobster season had closed. Of course, that didn't mean there weren't lobsters in the bag. Most of the fishermen "forgot" to bring in all of their traps. Fishing lobsters after the season closed was viewed much as bootlegging had been, illegal but not immoral. The close of the season on June 30 coincided with the arrival of the summer vacationers, all of whom were hungry for lobsters. With the season closed there were none, since in those days there were no pounds where the lobsters could be kept alive for later use. The only alternative was to get to know one of the fishermen well enough to arrange with him for some lobsters. At times when few people were on the jetty the transaction took place: two cars stopped side by side, a box quickly transferred from one trunk to the other, and payment made (the going rate that year was ninety cents per pound). The only telltale sign that lobsters had been obtained was the smell of lobster being cooked wafting from the chimney of the lucky buyers.

Nobody thought getting lobsters this way was wrong. I remembered back in 1958 when I answered a knock on the back door of our cottage about nine-thirty one night. There stood Sid Smith, then the president of the University of Toronto, a long-time friend and former colleague of my brother. He held a cardboard box in which there were four lobsters that he had just cooked. I don't think he had a guilty conscience; I know I didn't. They were delicious.

This activity was probably not a source of a significant amount of money for the fishermen. Maybe they might make enough to buy a few extras, like a bottle of rum. And they did have to be a bit circumspect as the Fisheries cutter appeared occasionally and cut loose any traps that "inadvertently" had been left behind after the season closed. But to the fishermen, the rewards were apparently worth the risks. To the economy of the Island, the service was important: the summer visitors had expected and wanted lobsters and there were none.

About ten after six, Emmett came sauntering down the wharf. I thought he looked about the same as he had in navy days, although a little grey showed at the temples. He was still that tall, lean man with a weather-beaten face and a peaked cap perched at a jaunty angle. His first words were "Good to see ya, Doc. Happy to get your call yesterday. Ready to go?"

"Sure am. You look great and you're not even drunk."

"Hell, no. You know I never take a drink."

"Sure, I know."

I looked down at the line of boats tied up below. "Which boat is yours?" There must have been ten or more boats, all looking much the same to my un-trained eyes and tied up, bow to stern, parallel to the wharf. The hulls seemed identical, about the same in length, and were painted either white or blue. All had a foredeck made of wood, a small cabin, and a winch mounted on the starboard gunnel. I no-ticed each owner had made minor variations to the superstructure, such as the size of the cabin or the positioning and shape of its windows.

"That one there, the *Sally Ann*, that's mine." Emmett pointed at the boat lying directly below us. "She's what the Nova Scotians call a 'Cape Islander.' You see its bow is higher than the others. The rest of the boats were made in various places around the Island, like Egmont or Freeland. *Sally Ann*'s thirty-two feet long and nine feet wide and her foredeck extends aft for eight feet. She's a great boat for lobster fishing, a real workboat. Later on I use her for mackerel and then cod. The cabin I built myself."

I thought the cabin looked as if a non-professional had built it, for the joints often did not fit and the wood used often mismatched. Open aft, it appeared to be little more than a shelter from the wind and dirty weather. The total absence of any creature comforts reinforced my impression this was a working boat. The wheel was located on the port side, attached to the aft upright of the cabin, at standing-man height. Amidship and athwartship lay a two-hundred-horsepower Ford engine. I soon found out the *Sally Ann* was Emmett's pride and joy. To me, she was a neat craft. She was tied in her place, but straining at her lines as the currents pushed and pulled. I felt that she, too, was eager to again experience the slow sensual surges of the open sea.

Emmett jumped the three or four feet down to the foredeck and looked up at me. "Coming?" he asked. I used the ladder. A few minutes later, he eased his boat out into the stream, made a hundred-and eighty-degree turn to starboard, and headed out the harbour. For at least a half-mile the channel was quite narrow and we went slowly, but once we passed the bell buoy, Emmett increased the speed of the motor. *Sally Ann* surged forward, her prow slicing the water. Emmett turned her westward, so we were traveling parallel to the coast. We began to feel the full effect of the ocean's roll; it was as I remembered it. Above the horizon the evening sky promised a fine day tomorrow.

I moved back to the stern and watched Emmett handle his craft.

About six feet tall, he was lean and muscular and his movements were quick and sure. Long exposure to the sun and the cold and the wind had leathered his skin. His dark brown hair, never quite under control, seemed compatible with light blue eyes that sparkled, flanked by laugh lines.

In a few minutes I walked up beside him. "This would've been a great boat to have had back in the bootlegging days."

"Sure would. But the boats we had then weren't that shabby. We could always outrun anything the Mounties could put up against us. That was always exciting."

"Why did you get involved in it? Weren't you ever worried about getting caught?"

"That didn't bother me. I didn't think there was much chance of that, 'cause we had better boats and we didn't think the Mounties were that smart. But the major reason I got into it was that the prices we were getting for fish were so low, we had to do something to get a few bucks just to survive. As for lobsters, in those days we were lucky to get twenty-five cents a pound. Often the market was so bad we spread them on the fields as a fertilizer. Anyway, our operation was so simple, it was hard to get caught. It was simply a matter of having a fast boat with a reliable engine, going out beyond the twelve-mile limit, exchanging recognition signals with the waiting schooner, and loading the boat to its gunnels with demerara. Then we'd head at full speed to the beach where we knew "friends" were waiting. Sometimes it got a bit hairy, like if it began to look as if there might be a trap. The whole thing was exciting, and in those days there wasn't much else that was. Besides, the rum was really good, the price right, and all our friends appreciated what we did."

A little while later, Emmett throttled back the engine. "Doc," he said, "there's a buoy dead ahead. When we get to it, catch it with this boat hook, will you?"

"Sure." I felt pleased he asked me to be more than a passenger.

The task was not very difficult. As the *Sally Ann* was coming to a stop beside a red and white buoy with a big black "W" painted across its top, I hooked the line and brought it on board. Emmett grabbed it, threw it around the winch, and engaged the clutch. I coiled the rope as it came on board; it seemed a reasonable thing to do.

Several traps were attached to this buoy's line. We pulled up one at a time, rested it on the gunwale, and removed any lobsters. There were about a half-dozen in the first three traps. "That's plenty for me," I said.

"You're sure?"

I nodded. Emmett put the lobsters in a plastic bag and carried them up to the cabin.

On the way back, he let me steer the *Sally Ann* until we reached the bell buoy. That was really a thrill. Standing on the port side by the cabin, holding the wheel firmly, I attempted to keep *Sally Ann* pointed towards a distant object up the coast. Sometimes she seemed to have a mind of her own and would suddenly, for no apparent reason, take off in another direction. As time went on I came to recognize her various impulses more quickly and corrected for them. I felt as if I were riding a spirited horse, enjoying her fire and excited by the challenge of having to control her.

We entered the harbour at a slow speed and headed towards the jetty. I noticed it was largely deserted. Ahead on the bluff by the Inn, a few people had gathered to watch the coming sunset. The clam-digging family had left and the rising tide now covered most of the sandbar. Immediately to my right, the boat trailer was empty and then I saw why. Emmett saw it, too, and at about the same time. The boat was in the water, heading towards us. Two men, dressed in dark brown uniforms, were in it. I felt my heart rate quicken.

"Christ!" Emmett muttered, and I noticed he altered our course just enough so we were no longer heading for the jetty, but running parallel to it on a line that would take us between the boat I had seen moored out in the stream and the shore. A moment later, he picked up the plastic bag containing the lobsters and walked back to where I was standing, the port side aft. He held it down below the gunwale so that *Sally Ann*'s side hid it from our interceptors. Dropping it at my feet, he whispered, "When we get so that boat ahead is between us and the Fisheries boat, drop it over the side."

I nodded. Now I understood why we hadn't continued on our course even though it risked being arrested "at sea" rather than when tied up at the wharf. We had to get rid of those lobsters!

Both the *Sally Ann* and the Fisheries boat continued at the same unhurried speed, parallel to each other. Finally we reached the cover of the moored fishing boat. I picked up the bag containing the lobsters and, making sure the men in the other boat could not see me, dropped it over the port side. As calmly as possible, I turned to see what was happening. Our pursuers were continuing to run abreast of us but at that moment, as I had hoped, were largely hidden by the boat lying between us. I gave a small sigh of relief. So far, so good.

Once we were past our cover boat, Emmett brought the *Sally Ann* around in a tight turn to starboard and headed at the same deliberate speed back towards the wharf. We met the Fisheries boat starboard to starboard. The officers looked at us, we at them. Nobody said a word. I glanced beyond them to where I had dropped the lobsters. My heart sank! There they were, floating jauntily in their plastic bag. God, I hoped the officers wouldn't turn around. I looked away so I wouldn't draw attention to them.

We tied up at the jetty with fore and aft lines. When the officers came alongside, Emmett and I turned to face them. They looked very serious, these two middle-aged men.

"You've been fishing lobsters out of season," the one in the middle of the boat said. The grey hair at his temples emphasized he was the older and he acted very much as if he were the senior officer. "We've been watching you, so when we saw you go out, we went up on the dunes on the other side and, with our binoculars, watched you the whole time you were out. We saw you pull the traps and we've got sightings. We know exactly where they are."

He paused. He had both Emmett's and my undivided attention. Emmett said nothing. Neither did I. I steadied myself against *Sally Ann*'s side, the one farthest away from the officers and nearest the jetty.

Emmett stood as if at attention, facing our accusers. He looked uncowed.

The officer continued. "Is the *Sally Ann* your boat?"

"Yes sir," Emmett replied, his voice firm.

The officer consulted a notebook he had taken from his pocket. "Then you be Emmett Robinson. Is that so?" The two officers exchanged knowing glances.

Emmett nodded.

"Our records show you have been caught poaching lobsters before. You know you could lose your lobster-fishing license because of this. Why don't you smarten up, for Christ's sake?" His voice was that of a father scolding a misbehaved adolescent.

"Where are those lobsters you got from those traps?"

"We don't have any lobsters. I was just taking my old friend from navy days for a little ride. Haven't seen him for a long time, ya know. Just a navy-style get-together."

Turning to the younger man, he said, "Go take a look. "

The junior officer climbed over *Sally Ann*'s gunwale and made a quick but thorough search. As far as I could see, she didn't have many hiding places.

"No. I can't find a single one," he said as he returned to his craft.

The senior officer looked surprised and disappointed. Turning to me, he looked me up and down. "As for you, it's a good thing you're a tourist or you'd be under arrest, too. Fishing lobsters out of season is illegal in Canada. We expect you to abide by our laws when you're a guest here." He said this with a firm steady voice. There was no question in my mind but that he meant every word. I thought it best not to tell him that although I was from away, I was still a Canadian citizen.

I kept silent but I felt awful. Here I was, getting off with only a scolding while Emmett, who depended on lobster fishing for the largest part of his income, was in danger of losing his license. I knew they were hard to get and he was in this position because of me. I didn't know what to say. He was watching the departing officers.

When they disappeared from sight, he came over to where I stood. "They're new here," he said. "Just trying to make a name for themselves, the bastards. Don't pay any attention to what those sons of bitches said. They're just tryin' to make you feel bad." With that he gave me a little jab in the shoulder and smiled.

"I'm really sorry, Emmett," I said, looking him in the eyes. "It's all my fault."

"Hell, just forget it. There's nothing to worry about. You only get wrinkles that way. It'll work out okay, you'll see." He glanced back to the mouth of the harbour. It was far too soon for the officers to return. "Guess I'd better tidy things up for the night."

"May I help?" I asked.

"No thanks. How about coming to my place for a drink tomorrow – about five o' clock?"

I began to feel better as Emmett didn't seem too worried. "Sure, that'd be great. See you at five."

I climbed the ladder, found my car, and drove the mile or so to my cottage. There, I decided not to say anything about it. It was too difficult to explain everything and I didn't like talking about it – not yet. I was still shaken for almost having been arrested.

The next afternoon at five, I parked my car as near Emmett's shack as I could and walked the remaining fifty yards or so. I knocked on the door and heard Emmett call out, "Come in." I did. He was alone.

It was about as simple a place as I could imagine, just one room, a table in the middle, three wood chairs, a double bed in the far right corner, and a kitchen area on the left. A window at the foot of the bed was the sole source of outside lighting, except for the door, when it was open. A naked light bulb hung in the centre of the room over the table.

The stubble on his face showed and I could smell rum on his breath as he greeted me at the door. Maybe he had been bothered more by yesterday's activities than he had let on or maybe he had just been celebrating the end of a successful lobster season a little late. I didn't ask.

"I've been over to Rustico and got a good supply of booze. Some good gin, too – Beefeater's. I suppose you'd like a pink gin, wouldn't you?" He said this with a trace of irony in his voice, a smile on his face. In the navy, a "pink gin" was a favourite drink in the officer's wardroom; the ratings got a tot of rum every morning at eleven. Emmett had been a rating, I an officer. I laughed. "No," I replied, "pink gins were never my piece of cake. I'd like a rum and coke, if you've got any coke."

We sat at the table for an hour or so, catching up on each other's doings and those of a few old friends from navy days. "I had an unusually good lobster season," he said, "but most of the guys were not as lucky, even worse than last year. Then in June, the

Fisheries Department had sent us all a special notice warning that we weren't to leave any traps out after the season ended. A conservation measure, they called it.

"Fisheries was concerned about 'overfishing,'" Emmett said. "The stupid bastards think that's why there were fewer lobsters this year. They'd forgotten that the new traps we started using this year have smaller entrances. The bigger lobsters can't get in; they're out there breeding. In another year or two there'll be lots of lobsters. We all expected a smaller catch this year. Nobody's surprised except the stupid Fisheries boys. It was their idea in the first place. You'd think they might've figured it out all by themselves, wouldn't ya? The stupid bastards! The few lobsters we poach each year don't make a difference, that's for sure. Hell, we just do that to help the summer visitors out."

He shook his head in disgust, got up, walked to the door, and looked towards the jetty. After a minute or so he came back, sat down, and picked up his glass. He rolled it slowly in his fingers, staring at the dark amber fluid. He looked immersed in thought. "Ya' know," he continued, speaking quietly, as if to himself, "they've made a lot of personnel changes, too. Some of my old friends in the department, like Bill Simpson, have been transferred off the Island and they've brought in new guys from away, ya' know, Nova Scotia and New Brunswick. Christ, do they take themselves seriously! And their jobs, too! They're always snoopin' around where they're not wanted. Islanders would never have acted like that. They understood what we were doing and why. These new guys are for the birds."

He sounded and looked more depressed than angry. After a pause, he went on, his voice dropping almost to a whisper. "It's not like the old days. Everything's gotten so damned serious and by the book."

From what I'd seen, I had to agree with him. The Fisheries Officers hadn't acted at all as if they were playing a game. As to whether there was a real conservation problem, I didn't know. Maybe poaching a few lobsters for the visitors was wrong; it certainly was illegal.

Neither of us said a word about yesterday until we had just about finished our second drink.

"The Fisheries boys came back last night a little while after you left. They had a couple of traps with them. I was still waiting in my boat."

Emmett said this as a simple statement of fact, without discernible emotion.

In a moment he went on. "They arrested me, the sons of bitches."

In one gulp, he downed the rest of his drink. Then he broke out a wide smile and started to chuckle.

"What's so funny?" I asked.

"I snookered them," he said. "Those traps they brought in were not mine. Mine have a big red 'R' painted on them, theirs a black 'W' and also the escape holes for small lobsters to get out are different. And they didn't find any lobsters, thanks to you. With no evidence, how can they convict me? Have another drink."

I felt my anxiety disappearing.

At the trial that fall, Emmett brought his own traps marked with a big red R. They were quite different from the ones the prosecution offered as evidence. And there weren't any lobsters.

Emmett was acquitted.

And let me tell you, even though I expected the acquittal, a great weight had been lifted off my shoulders.

CHAPTER FIFTEEN

I still remember the first time I saw her. It was in July 1945. Stuart Jones and I were walking down the main shopping street in Charlottetown, Prince Edward Island. A perfect summer's day, temperature in the mid-eighties, a few lazy cumulus clouds overhead, and a slight breeze. Because of gas rationing, there was little traffic and the cars that did pass were at least six years old as none had been made in Canada since the war began in 1939. So when a yellow four-door convertible sedan so clean and polished it looked like new came by, it attracted my attention. The rolled-down top revealed two attractive young blonde women, both dressed in white. Very chic, extremely attractive. For a moment I wondered if this was showing off the car or showing off these young women? Or both?

I not seen either of them before. They had not been among the young Island women who hung out with our young naval personnel. I turned to Stuart, a resident of the city, and asked, "Who are they?"

"They're the Large girls," he said. "The one that's driving, Gloria – but we all call her Sal or Sally – is said to be quite a character. The other one, Connie, I don't know that much about."

"What do you mean, quite a character?"

"For one thing, I've been told that Sal was overseas for at least two years in the Air Transport Auxiliary. Someone told me she'd even flown a plane across the Atlantic, but I doubt that story 'cause she's only seventeen or eighteen."

"What is the Air Transport Auxiliary?"

"They're a group of men and women pilots in Britain who fly replacement aircraft to wherever they're needed. Fighters, bombers whatever."

"Must be quite a woman to have done all that."

By July 1964, my wife, five children, our Siamese

cat, and I had become quite accustomed to making the four-day, 2,000-mile journey from our home in Iowa City, Iowa, to our summer rental cottage, simple but adequate, on Prince Edward Island. This was now the fourth year we'd made the trip. We enjoyed socializing with a group of friends who also loved the life at Stanhope on the north shore of the Island, facing the Gulf of St. Lawrence. We thoroughly enjoyed playing tennis four miles east at Dalvay Hotel, swimming in the brisk waters of the Gulf of St. Lawrence, soaking up the sun's rays on the sandy beach that stretched for miles in the National Park, and exploring the nearby brooks and rivers for trout. Our days were lived pleasantly.

But one mid-morning in early July, Charlotte Stevens, who always knew what was going on, announced to our group on the beach that Sally or Sal Large, now Walker, was going to join us shortly. Mmmm, I thought, I wonder if this might be the same Sally or Sal whom I'd seen in that yellow sedan in Charlottetown some twenty years before. Charlotte went on to tell the story how Sal had gone overseas, joined a group that flew replacement aircraft to where they were needed, and, when she came home, had received a hero's welcome. When

I heard that, I knew it must be the same person. While Charlotte went on to say that Sal had married again for the fifth time, the really important news was that Sal had bought that beautiful cottage back in the woods.

"This," I thought, "could be interesting."

Before long, Sal made her entrance. Appearing at the top of a sand dune some fifteen feet above us, this tall lean blonde, smiling broadly, waved to our group congregated on the beach below her. Her other hand held both a large blue parasol and the leash of a vigorous full-grown Doberman pinscher. In a moment or two she began to walk down the dune, one lithe step at a time. A tightly fitting one-piece blue bathing suit complemented her silver-blonde, casually curly hair and her tanned skin. Dare-devilish light-blue eyes dominated her face and said that life was for living. But in no way did she act seductively and, to me, one thing she lacked was sex appeal. In fact, she was sort of unisex, yet at the same time very attractive and very much a female. A very intriguing combination, I thought.

She had not come alone. Behind her followed the rest of her entourage, headed by a tall, striking, vigorous woman with dark hair and skin already deeply tanned. This was Stephanie, whom we learned was in charge of Sal's household. She held the leash of a second Doberman, this one a female. A third dog, an elderly Collie, ran loose. Then came the rest of Sal's family: the two foster boys, Shane and Stephen (the latter adopted in her first marriage), and three girls, Shannon, Sloan, and Sanna, all adopted since she married her newest husband, David Walker.

Even as Sal was meeting those of us she had not previously known, the pace and the spirit of the conversations picked up, as if, by her very presence, she had infused life and energy into the whole group.

Always physically vital, she listened actively, but also always seemed to have had a recent little adventure that she enjoyed sharing with us. I had difficulty believing many of her stories, but her ability to retell each story in exactly the same detail always added to its credibility.

Charlotte, one of our best friends and a woman who had a great sense of humour and who seemed to know everything worth knowing, told me quite a bit about Sal's past. "Sal's mother, Kay, is a very genteel woman, well-liked and respected in Charlottetown. She taught Sal how to sew and knit, as well as how to cook superbly and to entertain, all skills appropriate for a young woman whose presumed future role was that of wife and mother. But her father taught her her other skills. I don't know all the details, so you'll have to get Sal to tell you about them."

She abruptly stopped talking, got up, walked up and down for a minute or so, lit another cigarette, and then quickly sat down again. I thought she might have been making a decision.

This made me very curious, so a few days later when Anne and I visited Sal at her cottage, I said, "I've heard that your father was a very interesting man."

With that she got up and said, "I'm thirsty. I'm going to have a beer. How about you?"

"That'd be great."

Returning with two bottles of Molson's, Sal poured the beer into tall glasses and sat down. In some ways she reminded me of an actress relaxing after a show.

"Cheers," she said as she both sipped on her beer and took a long drag on a cigarette. "I don't suppose you know that I'm the second child in our family. My sister, Connie, was first and I'm pretty sure Dad wanted me to be a boy. When I turned out to be a girl, I guess he decided that for whatever reason there wasn't going to be a boy, so from the beginning he taught me all the things he would have taught his son, like plumbing, carpentry, and wiring a house – all sorts of things like that. When I was fifteen he taught me to fly in a de Havilland Moth, a little biplane. That was at the old Upton airport. I loved every minute of it. He'd learned to fly when he was in the Royal Flying Corps back in 1917. Anyway, in 1941, when I was seventeen, I went up to Ottawa, faked my age, and tried to enlist in the Royal Canadian Air Force."

"You did? You must have had a lot of nerve."

"I guess so, or maybe I just didn't know any better. Anyway, they said they were not enlisting any women, but they told me about the Air Transport Auxiliary. This was an organization of both male and female pilots in Britain who ferried all sorts of aircraft from depots to operational sites. In Montreal they tested my flying ability on Harvards, which were said to be hard to fly. I did okay, so they shipped me on the SS *Ivernia* over to the United Kingdom. There were only five Canadian female pilots in the organization, two of them from Toronto. I flew all sorts of planes, like Hurricanes and Spitfires and bombers like the Wellington Wimpy,

Lockheed Hudson, and Mosquito. It was everything I'd hoped for and I had a wonderful time. Some of the bigger aircraft, like Lancs, were difficult for me to fly because they required almost more strength than I had.

"Most of the time the flying was routine, but one time I thought my time was up. I was flying a new unarmed Spitfire from Eastleigh – that's near Southampton – to Biggin Hill, a very important airdrome near London. The flight was peaceful until one time when I looked around. There on my tail was a German Heinkel. I was helpless. Anytime he wanted he could shoot me down. What to do?"

Here she jumped up and stood erect, facing me, her right hand seizing the hair on the top of her head. "My feminine instinct took over. I yanked off my helmet and shook my blonde hair at him, smiled, and waved. You can believe I was relieved when he saluted, waggled his wings, and flew off."

During this whole episode, she looked intense, totally involved with the telling. Then she gradually relaxed down into her chair, her energy and emotions seemingly spent.

"My God, what a story! You did that?" I said. I felt I should have clapped.

She was silent for a few minutes. I wondered what she might say next. Finally she smiled and now, quite relaxed, said, "I had a great time, Life was so intense. Lots of parties. It was 'eat, drink, and make merry, for tomorrow – .' But it came to an end. I came home, was discharged in 1945 after a short visit home, I went to Florida and joined Macke Airlines, not as a pilot, but as a stewardess."

"When did this Spitfire event happen?" I asked.

"In the fall of 1943."

"I was at that airport in Eastleigh for a few weeks in the spring of 1944," I said. "At that time, I'm sure that Spitfires were not flown directly to fighter groups. I guess there must have been a lot of changes over those few months. Maybe your experience led to the change."

"Maybe so."

It'd been quite an afternoon and I thought it time we should leave. So I said,

"You've had some really amazing experiences and your family stories are fascinating. Neither of us have had to say a word, but you must be exhausted. We've got to go do some errands, but we'll get together again soon. And thanks for the beer. It hit the spot."

"Good," she said, smiling. "I'll tell you more about

me some other time, but now I've gotta go to the grocery store to get some food for my starving family. I look forward to seeing you again."

A few days later I saw her on the beach. She came over to where our family was sitting. "You know," she said, "I know hardly anyone here, so I'm going to have a lobster feed for any adult who wants to come at my cottage tomorrow about six. You'll come, of course."

The lobster season was closed locally and, as there were as yet no lobster pounds, I said, "Where are you going to get lobsters?"

"Piece of cake. They're flying them over from Newfoundland."

None of us were used to extravagance of that magnitude. Obviously, when Sal wants to have a party, she'd have a party and it'll probably be a doozer.

About ten the next morning, Shannon, Sal's oldest daughter, came to our cottage. She said her mother was ill and would I come to see her.

"I'm a pediatrician and I'm not used to looking after big people. Has she tried to get one of the other doctors? They'd be better than I."

"No, she wants you."

After I made myself somewhat presentable, I walked the half-mile or so to her cottage. As usual, the two ferocious Dobermans, barking furiously, met me as I walked through the gate; they still scared me every time I was near them. Sal was lying in bed and complaining of severe abdominal pain and some vomiting. She told me that recurrently she had bouts of pancreatitis and that's what she thought she had now. That was not something that I, a pediatrician, had any experience with. After I examined her, I thought my findings were more suggestive of gastritis. She looked so pale and worn out I couldn't see how she could put on a party in a few hours and I told her so. "Why don't you postpone it until tomorrow?"

"No way!" she said, "I can do it. Just you wait and see." Her voice seemed much stronger than when I first began talking to her. "Don't even tell anyone I've had this little upset. I have medicine I've used before when I've had this. It'll work." Those instructions were uttered very firmly.

I left, wondering why she'd had me come to see her.

At six o'clock, Anne and I walked over to Sal's cottage. The dogs were nowhere to be seen, but the odour of lobster being cooked filled the air. A few of our friends were already there and had been helping themselves to the huge array of hard liquors and wines on a table near the entrance. I walked through to the kitchen. There David, whom I'd not previously met, and some ten years younger than Sal, and Steffi were happily steaming the lobster and finishing off the other preparations. I had never seen such an array of lobsters, some still alive, crawling around aimlessly, others already cooked, piled on large plates, on shelves – anywhere there was a space for them.

Finally when they were finished with the cooking, David arranged them on the ten-foot-long rectangular dining room table. What an extraordinary sight. These beautiful big red lobsters, piled one on top of another, covered the entire table. They were much the same size; all weighed at least two pounds, appearing much bigger than the ones usually sold as "markets." Two different salads, newly made homemade bread, melted butter, and mayonnaise completed the main course. For those still capable, fresh green-apple pie and ice cream stood by at the ready. "Eat and drink as much as you want." Those were Sal's orders and no one failed to heed them.

At this moment Sal made her appearance looking

as if she had never been ill her whole life. Full of pep and energy, she was the perfect hostess. How she did it, I have no idea.

The following summer, 1965, the wives and children of our Stanhope social group by design arrived at Stanhope about a week before us husbands. They said their plan was to busy themselves opening their cottages and getting provisions in preparation for what they expected to be an active summer season. They'd expected Sal would be there, but after almost the week had gone, she hadn't showed.

Soon after I arrived, my wife, Anne, could hardly wait to tell me about the wonderful adventure they'd all had just the previous Saturday. This is what she said.

"Sit down and I'll tell you about it. Just be quiet until I finish. Okay?"

I got myself a cup of coffee and sat down on the sofa. I was ready to listen.

Anne began, "We were down on the beach sunning ourselves and talking, when Sal's sister, Connie, spotted the missing member of the group. 'Here she comes now. Thank God, she's got Lassie with her, not that Doberman. Lassie's okay, but I still prefer the Pekingese.'"

"You know, dear," Anne said to me, "that the two sisters frequently disagree."

I nodded.

"All of us, Charlotte and Claire and Ruth and I, immediately rolled over from our stomachs and sat up to watch Sal.

"'Good,' Claire said. 'She'll have some ideas for tonight. The men will be coming in a few days and I'd sure like to do something exciting without them being around.'

"We all nodded. Not much had been happening since we'd arrived that was unusual. We'd all opened our summer cottages and gotten in some food and some beach time, so that we were happy with the progress of our tanning. We were relatively free, for all our children are old enough that they don't have to be looked after very much any more, and the area's so safe we all felt we could leave them and not worry. But what was there for us to do? Maybe Sal could suggest something. We hoped so.

"As soon as she got near, Sal called out to us, 'Great to see you all again.'

"She also waved to others farther down the beach and then sat down with us. She began by saying,

'Are you girls ready for some fun tonight? Our husbands aren't around, so let's have some *Just Women Fun* on our own.'

"'That's what we were talking about just before you arrived,' Charlotte said. 'The men will be coming soon, so let's be at it.'

"'Good,' Sal said. Then she went on to tell us that now there's a new restaurant in Montague called the Lobster Shanty North. Apparently the owner, a former Islander, has a Lobster Shanty South in New Jersey somewhere. This one's only about thirty-five miles away. 'We can go there and find out whether it's any good or not. How about it?'

"Charlotte said that it sounded great to her and the rest of us nodded our agreement. We then decided we'd dress up for the occasion, getting out of our cottage-cleaning grubbies. We were to meet at Sal's at seven.

"Promptly at that hour we converged on Sal's cottage. Showered, perfumed, coiffured, make-up in place, evening gowned and high-heeled, we were ready for a party as we walked across the unmowed field and up the gravel path to Sal's. We were ready for a night out on our own, with none of you husbands around to bother us.

"The drive to Montague went smoothly. Of course, Sal drove, and, as usual, with verve. The restaurant itself was a pleasant surprise. Quite large with a lovely view of the river; it was appropriately rustic. More importantly, the lobsters were superb, the drinks stimulating. For dessert, we all decided to have strawberry shortcake, topped off with what they called 'liquid fire,' Drambuie. Have you ever tasted it, Charles?"

"Yes, it's special," I said.

"The engine purred softly in the night air as Sal drove slowly back to Stanhope. All of us women, warmed by our carefree evening with good friends, good food, and lots to drink, were relaxed and enjoying the ride back to the cottages.

"'It's such a beautiful night,' Sal commented.

"And it was. I was so impressed that I pointed out that there was not a cloud in a star-strewn sky that stretched from horizon to horizon, that the Milky Way was like a thick blanket strewn across its midriff, and that the full moon illuminated the countryside so brightly that it was almost as if it were daytime. We five women traveled in silence, all of us apparently enjoying the ambiance of the evening.

"Sal's voice suddenly interrupted the silence. 'Look

at that field over there on the right. See how it's completely covered in daisies. Isn't that spectacular!'

"She slowed the car, and then stopped it entirely. Daisies filled the field from the edge of the black top to the spruce trees in the far distance. In the moonlight they appeared as myriad lit white candles gently swaying in the summer's night breeze.

"'Let's go in!' Sal cried enthusiastically. 'Let's go dance with the daisies.'

"Connie piped up, 'I don't think we should. It's not our field and the farmer might not like it. Anyway, it's really late and I'm tired.'

"'You're always against everything, Connie.' Sal replied. 'Why don't you just relax for once and enjoy this incredible night?'

"With that, Sal jumped out of the car, swung open the gate with a flourish, got back in the car, and drove gaily into the field.

"'It's like being in the middle of a big garden, isn't it? What a gorgeous sight,' Charlotte bubbled.

"Suddenly the car began to struggle, its progress slowed. Sal gunned the engine. It stalled.

"'See,' cried Connie. 'I told you so. Get it going again, Sal. You can always fix everything. Now fix this.' Her voice sounded more than a little hysterical.

"Sal said nothing for a minute or two. Then she said, 'Something is seriously wrong with the car, something unusual, something I've never experienced before.

"'Well, it's no use sitting here, girls. Let's take a look and see if we can find out what's wrong.'

"We got out of the car in our heels and long dresses, daisies up to our knees. Sal lifted the hood and inspected the engine.

"Meanwhile Connie looked under the car. 'My God, we're caught in a net, a big fishing net, the kind they use to catch mackerel,' she wailed. 'Some fisherman must have laid his net out to dry overnight and it's wrapped around what I think is called a drive shaft. I'll bet you've never been caught in a net in a field of daisies before, Sal. How are you going to get yourself out of this one?'

"'Not a problem,' Sal replied very matter-of-factly. 'I know the guy who owns this field. Doesn't do much farming. That's why there's so many daisies. They don't make very good hay. Mostly he fishes lobsters in the spring season, cod and mackerel after that. He just lives up the road. I'll go get him.'

"Out the gate she went, turned left, and walked up the gravel road, high heels and all. We waited, wondering what was going to happen next.

"Before long she was back, the owner with her. A jovial type, he greeted us women with a big smile. 'Never caught so many beautiful fish before. I'll get you out of here in no time at all.'

"With that he disappeared under the car, and when he emerged, the net was untangled. 'Many thanks.' We all got back in the car and off we went. But what an adventure we'd had."

Anne told me all about it very dramatically, even mimicking the voices in the various comments that had been made. I think she and all the wives were pleased not only to have such an adventure, but also to have such an amusing story to tell us men.

Sal was always ready for a party, but the most elaborate by far was the cocktail party she had at her home in Charlottetown, a large ornate Victorian mansion on West Streeet. The ostensible reason for the party was to celebrate my forty-seventh birthday. We went expecting it would be over by seven-thirty or eight. I didn't know that there were 356 invitees. They began to arrive at five-thirty; the last two to leave, at two-thirty in the morning, were the Premier and the Lieutenant Governor of Prince Edward

Island, both of them in a very convivial mood. I can't imagine how much liquor and how much food these guests must have consumed. Who was the centrepiece of the party? Sal, of course. She was everywhere, knew everyone, and made sure everything ran smoothly.

Somehow I couldn't make sense of this party. Was it to show me off to these apparent leading persons in Charlottetown society? I didn't think of myself as a "name," whereby her position in Charlottetown society would be magnified. Perhaps it was to show me how many important people she knew, but that didn't make any sense to me either. Finally I decided my birthday was just an excuse for a party.

The party seemed to set the stage for the rest of the summer, for there were more social activities than we experienced either before or ever again. Family tennis daily at nearby Dalvay, swimming and walking and games on the beach, digging clams, and such games as "Run sheep, run" and "Hearts" (on rainy days) filled the daylight hours. Horse harness racing in a country track not far from our cottage held our interest one Wednesday. In the evenings, I often tried my hand at trying to catch the always elusive trout, while my children frequently went up to the nearby Centre in the evenings where Gordon Lightfoot, not yet famous, provided free entertainment. On many evenings Anne and I played bridge with Harry and Ruth Younker, or increasingly with Sal and David. She was always my partner and became a very good player. I became convinced that although she was not very well-educated, she was damned intelligent. It seemed that any role she chose to play, she did well.

When we arrived at Stanhope the following year, 1966, we found there had been a major change. Sal had rented her cottage and was now living in Charlottetown. That meant we saw little of her, for now she was heavily involved with managing the cottages she owned at Savage Harbour and at Silver Sands on the bay shore at Stanhope.

The last time I saw Sal was some years later, in 1988. I'd heard that the city of Charlottetown had recognized her wartime achievements the previous fall and that it had been on the local television. No longer was she living in her beautiful family home on West Street, but in a more modest house on Rochford Street. I knocked on the door. Her son answered and showed me to the parlour where his mother was sitting in the middle of à leather sofa. She recognized me and gave me a halfhearted welcome, which I felt was probably all she was capable of, for she looked so thin and enervated, a pale shadow of her former self. I tried to talk with her but it was difficult, for her responses consisted almost entirely of single words. Finally she strongly indicated to me that it was very important to her that I see the video that had been made the previous fall on November 11, Armistice Day, when a local television program recognized her wartime activities. It lasted but a few minutes. We watched it together silently.

I'd been told that she'd had a stroke in 1981 and was said to never have been the same thereafter. Only a few months after I last saw her, she had another stroke and died.

Addendum

Lettice Curtis, an Englishwoman who published an accurate history of the Air Transport Auxiliary, *The Forgotten Pilots*, recorded Gloria Walker as having been in Britain from the 5th of July 1942 to the 21st of September of the same year. Gloria was a Cadet, a pilot in training. More recently, Shirley Render corroborated Ms. Curtis's account in her book, *No Place for a Lady*. She commented that Gloria was a great party girl, but was never in an airplane. But what a wonderful story she'd made of it.

AFTERWORD

As soon as I retired from the navy in January 1946, I returned to Montreal as planned, and became a Resident Physician in the Montreal Children's Hospital. I soon became intrigued by the multiple problems presented by one of my patients, the newly born infant of a diabetic mother. This led to my becoming a graduate student in Experimental Medicine at McGill, a Fellow of the hospital, and the next year the Rutherford Fellow of McGill University. During this period I was able to show that normal newborns have normal adrenal cortex function and are able to respond appropriately to stress, such as pneumonia. This was not previously known. These studies also showed that increased adrenal activity was not the cause of the problems seen in infants of diabetic mothers.

With the financial support of the Commonwealth Foundation in New York, I spent 1949-50 as a Fellow at Harvard Medical School in Pediatrics at the Massachusetts General Hospital and Harvard Medical School, attempting to develop methods to measure human pituitary growth hormone and insulin. These were unsuccessful, but I had a great learning experience in this environment.

In 1951 I became an assistant professor in Paediatrics at the University of Manitoba's Winnipeg Children's Hospital. Not knowing that I'd spent the last few years largely in laboratories, I was asked to be in charge of the diabetic service. I thought that even though I had never seen a child with diabetes or had any lectures on the subject, except for exceptional instruction on how to treat the most serious complication (acidosis), I accepted this challenge. At that time the diet for diabetics was very complicated and I found that both the diabetic children and their parents had real difficulty following it. I wondered if I could follow it, even though it was generally accepted as being the one and only truth. I saw that it was not scientifically sound and devised a new one based only on the carbohydrate content of the food. I called this the Constant Carbohydrate diet. Today this is the basis of all diets for diabetics. Of course I was able to do this because I didn't have to unlearn anything I'd been taught earlier – I had an empty head.

In the laboratory I continued working on an assay for insulin. Clinically I did general hospital-based paediatrics and endocrinology. With the help of Dr. Sid Israels, I re-organized the residency program. It grew from two rotating residents from the General Hospital to twelve full-timers in 1954. We also updated the way in which laboratory tests were reported.

Because of the difficulty I had in raising money to support my research and my inadequate salary, in 1954 I accepted an associate professorship and in 1959 a full professorship at the University of Iowa Medical College in Iowa City, Iowa. There I had good laboratory and financial support so that I was able to hire a lab technician and again began working on an insulin assay which we finally achieved in

1962. That was all to no avail because a much simpler assay was then being used. However I started up the Pituitary Growth Hormone study again in 1956 when pure Growth Hormone became available and an assay for insulin using an antibody was described. I thought that should work for Growth Hormone, too, and two years later we had such an assay. That year and the next few years it attracted worldwide attention but a similar assay using a radioactive tag soon appeared. It was much simpler to use and soon replaced our assay. Those investigators rightfully won the Nobel Prize; I was told I was nominated, but I doubt that.

From the beginning I was in charge of the diabetes program. Feeling strongly that children and their families needed to know how to cope with managing their problem, I developed a team consisting of a nurse educator, a dietitian, and me, and taught each of our patients how to look after their problem. By 1965 I was sufficiently concerned about the role of fat in causing atherosclerosis that I lowered the fat content to thirty per cent. In due course I became the first president of the Iowa Affiliate of the American Diabetes Association and then a Director of that national organization.

I also did a thirty-six-year study that demonstrated that treating hyperthyroidism in young people with radioactive iodine is both effective and safe.

Virtually every summer in all those years, my family and I drove the 2,000 miles from Iowa City so we could spend a month vacationing at Stanhope. We had a great time: tennis at Dalvay, swimming, fishing, and playing games; and we enjoyed Island activities, the beautiful countryside, the other vacationers at Stanhope, and the Island people.